CAREERSCAN

CAREERSCAN

How to Advance Your Career

Edward H. Scissons, Ph.D.

DEMBNER BOOKS
New York

DEMBNER BOOKS
Published by Red Dembner Enterprises Corp., 80 Eighth Avenue, New York, N.Y. 10011
Distributed by W. W. Norton & Company, Inc., 500 Fifth Avenue, New York, N.Y. 10110

Library of Congress Cataloging in Publication Data

Scissons, Edward H.
 CareerScan: how to advance your career.

 Includes index.
 1. Vocational guidance—Programmed instruction.
I. Title. II. Title: Career scan.
HF5381.S446 1985   650.1'4'077   85-4503
ISBN 0-934878-64-1
ISBN 0-934878-65-X (pbk.)
Designed by HELGA MAASS GRAPHIC DESIGN

CareerScan is dedicated to the memory of J. Edward Scissons, a man who loved his work.

Preface

CareerScan could not have been written were it not for the generous contribution of others. Thanks are due to Lorraine Blashill, Karen Dellow, Glenis Joyce, and Al Fraser for their helpful comments and suggestions. Isobel Findlay was most professional in reviewing the original manuscript.

Special thanks are due to Diane Harris, my editor at Dembner Books, for her lucid suggestions (and sharp pencil), and to Red Dembner for believing in CareerScan.

Finally recognition must be given to the many individuals and organizations that have permitted me to formulate and refine the techniques outlined in CareerScan—at their expense.

CONTENTS

Introduction

"No man can give another the capacity to think. Yet that capacity is our only means to survival."—*For the New Intellectual* by Ayn Rand

There are many of us whose career depends on your career. We have been telling you how and what to decide about your life, the importance of a logical and planned career path, how to integrate career goals with larger life interests, how to be fulfilled in your job, etc. If you took all our advice, you would be too busy managing your career to work!

Like any developing field, career assistance services is plagued by an insatiable thirst—a thirst to include every possible variable that is or may be related to your career. Perhaps because each of us who works in the area develops a particular interest (mine happens to be the assessment of abilities), the sum total of what is presented to the consumer becomes mind-boggling. To be glib, there are two choices: to work your way through a never ending array of career how-to's or to forget the whole thing and just let your career happen. If until now you have chosen the second, you are following a path traveled by a great many others—including most of the experts.

I have a confession to make. My career is unplanned, uncertain, and I am not really sure about how it fits in with my life goal. In fact, I do not have a life goal. Much of my career is a result of capitalizing on accident, happenstance, or plain good luck. Not that I did not do my part, but I sure did not plan it. And there are many others like me. I do not know any people who

1

planned their careers the way they were supposed to, who practiced the logical, planned, or prescriptive techniques so much in vogue today. Everybody that I would call successful—and happy—has been doing it wrong.

Unfortunately much writing and preaching in the career field suffers from a major fault: confusing how people actually develop careers or select jobs with how the writer thinks they should. Your career success to date, you are led to believe, has occurred in spite of your haphazard approach. You are lucky you got as far as you did without "doing it right." Yet the fact is many career development methods are ridiculously complex, tedious, removed from the reality of what people actually do, or plain silly. As a consequence no one follows them.

Generally such methods focus on the establishment of life and career goals and a lock-step plan to reach these goals. Career success, you are told, is what you will get to rather than what you can have today. Unfortunately a career or life based solely on such end goals is a long-term mortgage on a progressively deteriorating piece of property.

Your life goal will be where you end up based on how you respond to the opportunities you create or recognize as they come your way. If you are not satisfied with how you are going, you will be no more satisfied with where you end up.

In an interview Lorraine asked for help to get where she wanted to go. What she needed was help in enjoying where she was.

Lorraine had no present. She had traded it for a glorious future. When she was in high school, she hated it but dreamed of college. College was tolerated only because it led to a job in marketing. Her junior marketing position was a bore but she dreamed of an executive position. Each successive career stage was enjoyable only for what it might lead to.

Fortunately you can live in the present *and* move forward in your career. If you are like most people, you manage your career by responding to opportunities or chance events that come your way. You select your career path by making decisions about whether or not a particular opportunity will be good for you. Not only is this the way you start out planning your career, but even after you have honed your methods, you probably will continue—no matter what advice the many career management how-to books you read give. To be successful, career development methods must fit with what you are already doing—and improve upon your own methods.

The important aspects of managing your career are neither complex nor lengthy. You do not need to have every part of your life in well balanced harmony in order to have a successful career. You do not have to make nearly impossible decisions about future courses of action. You do not need to be absolutely certain about anything. What you do need are practical tactics for recognizing your priorities and for going after what you decide you want.

To be successful in managing your career, you need only to commit yourself to think through alternatives that could improve on what you are already doing, that show you how to capitalize on your own strengths so you can take full advantage of the opportunities around you. I call this approach logical career management.

My goal for you in this book is to improve the quality of your career decision-making. Like any good teacher, I will do that by asking the kinds of questions that will point you in the right direction for you. I'll also deal with the possible actions that you may choose to take and the implications of such actions.

Material presented in this book was developed and refined in countless workshops, seminars, and individual consultations I have conducted with individuals seeking to improve their careers. Participants have ranged from senior executive officers of major international corporations to unemployed bank clerks. The approach works only because these brave souls have made it work. I gladly share the credit with them.

3

WHAT IS CAREER MANAGEMENT?

There are three naturally occurring stages of career management. That is, they happen whether or not you pay attention to them, whether or not you make conscious decisions. These stages form the substance of CareerScan.

1. What place is a job going to occupy in your total life and at different points in your life?

As far as your life is concerned, a job can be everything or nothing, although it is seldom either extreme. In Section I of CareerScan I will focus on helping you to identify what your life needs are and what part a job might play in meeting these needs.

2. If a job is important in helping you meet your needs, how do you identify what jobs will be best for you?

I will deal with a method in Section II that will help you select the best kind of job for you. I will focus on assessing your abilities—as well as balancing what you want and need with what you are likely to get.

3. How can you get the job you need?

For many, searching for a job is their only contact with career management, the only job how-to they ever pursue. In Section III I'll deal with job-search techniques and detail a practical, no-nonsense approach to getting the job you choose.

WHO SHOULD READ CAREERSCAN?

If you have done any reading in the field of career management or perused any of the how-to books dealing with job-search skills, you know that there are a great many to choose from. Generally these books purport to be applicable to everyone: the student, the blue-collar worker, the senior manager. I make no such claim.

This book is not intended for the inexperienced high school or college student. I have clearly aimed the content of this book at experienced professionals or white-collar workers who wish to improve their career path. It is not necessary that your experience be recent or in an area that you intend to pursue; it is important that you have some employment experience to use this book to best advantage.

HOW TO READ CAREERSCAN

This book was not written sequentially to end and there is little necessity for you to read it that way. In fact there may be no reason for you to read the entire book. What you should read depends on where you are in your particular life and career. Perhaps your career is at a turning point, or you are uncertain where to go or exactly why you want to get to a specific goal. Perhaps you are just starting your career again after a lengthy absence. If your situation is like these, start with Section I.

Perhaps you know what you want out of work but need some help in determining what you have to offer, your abilities and talents. If that is the case, skip the beginning and start with Section II.

Perhaps you already know what you want and what you have to offer (or these are not immediate concerns) but need some help in improving your skills to get a new job. Section III is for you.

For further guidance in deciding which of the three sections of CareerScan you would find valuable, refer to the questions at the start of each section. They provide the best guidelines.

Remember that there are few rules in career management that cannot be broken and even fewer that ought not to be broken in certain instances. It is your career, so if you disagree with anything you read in this book, trust your own judgment. You will not be comfortable doing something you do not agree with. What is important is that whatever you do in managing your career it be what you have chosen. Many times we deny ourselves the action necessary to effect real change because we do not truly believe in the method we are using, are reluctant to admit this to ourselves, and translate this nonbelief into nonaction. For a system to work, you must make it your own. *CareerScan* has been designed to make that possible. There is no need to wait for someone else to convince you of the right way to go about doing things when you can adopt the techniques offered here and move forward on your own.

Good luck.

SECTION I

Career Versus Life

"The question of the meaning of life can be approached in various ways. . . . We must first determine whether it is even permissible to ask about the meaning of the whole, whether such a question itself is meaningful."
—*The Doctor and the Soul* by Viktor Frankl

— you are uncertain about the place a career should have in your life.
— you are thinking of returning to work after a lengthy absence.
— you have reached most of your career goals and are wondering where to go from here.
— you find yourself increasingly less interested in your work and more interested in nonwork pursuits.
— you can see that the work you do is interesting but you find little satisfaction in it.
— you are at a career change point: promotion, transfer, termination, etc.
— you want to know more about yourself and what a career can offer you.

SKIP THIS SECTION IF . . .

— you are fairly certain what you want out of work.
— you are desperate to find a job and cannot take the time to get your life in order.
— you are not prepared to make hard decisions and compromises about what you want.
— your life is in total chaos and you are looking for the answer.

Chapter 1

A Career—Why Bother?

"I have, let's say, sixty years to live. Most of that time will be spent working. I've chosen the work I want to do. If I find no joy in it, then I'm only condemning myself to sixty years of torture."—Howard Rourk in *The Fountainhead* by Ayn Rand

If we are to believe the popular or academic press, there is a crisis in employment, in working. On the one hand many people are working at jobs they find increasingly meaningless, boring, and dehumanizing. On the other hand, one in every ten North Americans who wants a job cannot find one, a situation unlikely to be substantially alleviated within the next decade. According to Daniel Yankelovich in *New Rules*, this has resulted in a sour grapes I-can't-do-anything-about-it attitude on the part of many workers. They are damned if they cannot work and damned if they do.

Given this disheartening scenario, what is the place of logical career management? Why bother to become employed if the only job you are likely to get will make you throw up your hands in despair. Maybe the only sensible decision is to forget decisions.

I do not feel that the career world is as bleak as the media presents it. Nor do I think that getting and keeping a fulfilling and meaningful job is as impossible as is often thought.

The long-term danger with the scenario outlined above is not the grim statistics, nor the broken lives of the unemployed. *The long-term danger is the erosion of a belief in the absolute necessity of individual decision-making and responsibility.* The danger is that in blaming circumstance for the present dilemma, it is left to circumstance to improve things.

Jobs are difficult to find. Satisfying jobs are even more difficult to find and keep. But there are jobs—good ones—available each and every day in North America. They may not be there ripe for the picking—but they are there.

As far as unemployment or worker satisfaction is concerned, what the popular press says offers the clearest example of how to lie with statistics. A ten percent unemployment figure or a twenty, thirty, or forty percent worker dissatisfaction figure still translates into a ninety percent employment figure and an eighty, seventy, or sixty percent worker satisfaction level. Believing that the *un* or *dis* figures accurately represent the state of North American work is like believing that the Sunday morning TV preacher accurately represents the state of North American religion.

Everybody does not need to find a job—or a fulfilling job—for you to find one. The odds for gratifying employment are not perfect, but they are in your favor. If you want a job, even if you want a particular kind of job, and if you are qualified, you have a far better than even probability of getting it. But you must decide you want it and commit yourself to some process in order to get it. To be successful, you must take charge of your own circumstances, capitalize on your natural advantage.

Arne was a hard rock geologist, three years out of school when the slump in the mining industry hit. The unemployment rate in his industry was thirty-five percent, and in his part of the country it was even worse. Arne knew what he wanted, a computer applications job within geology. It was a job he had only imagined, requiring a thorough knowledge of geology as well as a detailed knowledge of how computers might be used for integration of geological data. If there were few jobs in geology, there would be even fewer in specialized and speculative branches of the field.

Arne mapped out a plan. He would approach small entrepreneurial consulting geological companies with his idea, appeal to them on the basis of a ground floor opportunity to make money. It took some selling (and a lot of legwork) before he found someone who was willing to chance his "wild" ideas. Today he is a successful co-owner of a highly specialized geological consulting company. The unemployment rate in his industry is still high.

But I am getting ahead of myself. If you are reading this section, your first concern is not with the mechanics of getting a meaningful job but with deciding if you want a career—and if so, what you want it to give you. A career after all is something more than a lifetime's random collection of jobs. A career implies some purposeful relationship between jobs—and that may not be for you. To have a career you have to understand the perspective of your job. You need to know where work fits with all of the other things you want or do not want to do with your life. For you, the question may be . . .

A CAREER—WHY BOTHER?

There are two main reasons to consider working. One is that you may have to in order to enjoy eating regularly. The other is that you may choose to in order to maintain your sanity. Most people probably work for both reasons, although the weighting in favor of one or the other varies throughout life. As Ralph Weinrich so aptly puts it in the *Michigan Business Review*, "Let us stop equating work with earning a living but rather think of it as an an important component of making a life."

It is common to envy people who work because they want to in contrast with those who work because they have little choice. But is such envy justified? Probably not. There is no reason to believe that, given the fact that you have to work, your work must be any less rewarding or enjoyable than someone who works by choice. Your present job may not be enjoyable, but work itself can offer you the same thing it offers those who select it freely—satisfaction.

Mark was a twenty-nine-year-old engineer, unhappy with his job, seemingly with work itself for no particular reason. He was the eldest son of previously wealthy parents who had lost everything in a business failure when Mark was nineteen.

"I just don't like the idea of having to work. I never thought I would work for somebody, or at least that I would have to," he said in interview.

When asked what he would be doing if his parents had not lost their fortune, he sat in thought a long while. Finally he replied, "Engineering, I guess."

The satisfaction that can come from work is the same type of satisfaction that can come from any area of life. It is the feeling you get when you are doing what is necessary to meet your needs. But it is knowledge of those needs, knowledge of you, that is important if you are to clarify the place of work in your life.

Ken managed the purchasing operation for a national chain of discount consumer stores. It was a cut-throat business and he loved it. Very often profit was made on the slimmest of margins. Wringing an extra three percent discount at his end of the operation often made the difference between making or losing money for the company.

Ken enjoyed making money—and beating others in order to do it. He was very successful at both.

Unknown to most of his associates, Ken was also a tireless worker in a charity providing assistance to fatherless boys. He contributed time and money freely, was the one person who could always be counted on to help. Ken received little apparent recognition for his help but claimed that for him "it made everything seem worthwhile."

Work can be everything or nothing and you can still be happy. You can maximize that happiness by deciding what place work will occupy in your life and, if you do work, by selecting work that meets your needs.

YOU . . .

It is hard to talk about your job, your career, without talking about you. I do not know too much about you. Perhaps you do not either. To go through what we have to in this section, you will have to do some serious thinking about yourself.

What are you like? What kinds of experiences have you had? What makes you happy? How much energy do you have? Do you like bagels? As Plato said, "Know thyself." (More about this later because career-wise he was only half-right.) The basis of decision-making is information. In the case of career decision-making, the information that is most important concerns you.

What is important about you when it comes to deciding the place a career will have in your life are your needs and what you will do to meet those needs.

Needs range from the basic human requirements shared by everyone to sophisticated personal or life-style preferences. Obviously we all have primary requirements such as food, shelter, and safety that have to be met. But beyond those we have varying needs for such things as social contact, self-esteem, and personal fulfillment, what Rollo May calls our moral duty to develop ourselves. As soon as we get beyond the basic biological level, we discover a whole range of preferences and wants that are different for each of us. One person may need more physical activity, another more companionship, another more artistic expression. No one is the same as anyone else, and there is little sense in acting as if you are.

13

Needs are important because they form a major basis for your behavior. What you decide to do is a concrete manifestation of an underlying need. You act in order to express a need or attempt to reduce its intensity.

Often you have needs you are unaware of because they are satisfied. For example, you may have a strong personal need for affection and since you have a loving relationship with a mate or with friends, you do not think about that need. In that case your love-seeking behavior would probably be minimal. That particular need is being met.

But all of us have a variety of different needs and this helps to explain a good deal about our internal conflicts—tensions, anxiety, or stress. Such unpleasant feelings are often the result of unmet needs or of a conflict between two or more needs: the "having your cake and eating it too" dilemma.

Needs are long-lived. Behavior, on the other hand, changes with natural changes in your life. What happens to the strong need for love when your spouse dies, your best friend moves away, or you are forced to relocate thousands of miles from your roots? Probably you do something different when confronted with these changes. You'll exhibit some behavior that seeks to regain a balance.

Al was always known at work as a quiet but very competent worker. He seldom socialized with the other employees during or after working hours, was very work oriented when he was at work.

Al's wife of seventeen years died after a brief illness. After a short absence Al returned to work.

Changes were soon evident in Al's personality and style in dealing with others. He would often stop and talk with others, sometimes interrupting their work to do so. At a staff meeting he volunteered to coordinate the Christmas party, an event he had never attended before. He seemed to spend a great deal of effort seeking approval from others for his work, which was always first-class.

In some ways many preferred the old Al to this new social gadfly.

When you find yourself changing your behavior or experiencing inclinations for change, look for losses or gains in your life before you look for changes in your needs.

Your career can help to meet your needs, conflict with your needs, or remain apart from your needs. As far as your needs are concerned, the more you know about them, especially which are most important, the more you can mold your work and other activities to them.

In *CareerScan* there are no shoulds for your needs. Instead there are proven exercises that help you to identify your own needs and to rate them in terms of their importance in your life.

Chapter 2

Needs and Your Career

"From each according to his abilities, to each according to his needs."—The Criticism of the Gotha Program by Karl Marx

We are all capable of a wide range of behavior. For ease of understanding we often categorize behavior—religious behavior, sexual behavior, political behavior, work behavior, and so on, even though the same action may be done in each case. You might work at a job that fulfills your need for helping others or you might work out that need by a rich religious or political avocation.

A career provides one opportunity to meet your needs. In planning your career the two critical questions are, "What are your needs and how will you choose to act them out?"

WHAT ARE YOUR NEEDS?

Perhaps you already have a good handle on your own needs, a good knowledge of yourself and what you are about. Perhaps you already know if your needs are in conflict with one another and have made your trade-offs in resolving these conflicts. Perhaps, but not likely.

The range of possible human needs is limited only by your imagination. Let us look at a few commonly accepted ones:

1. *Influence:* You like to be in a position to change the attitudes or alter the opinions of others.

2. *Altruism:* It is important for you to help other people by your actions, either alone or in groups.

3. *Affiliation:* You desire feelings of closeness and similarity with a group of people or organization.

4. *Competition:* You find it pleasurable to engage in activities where you are trying to outperform others.

5. *Intellect:* You achieve feelings of satisfaction by thinking through problems or developing courses of action.

6. *Aesthetics:* Creation or appreciation of things of beauty is meaningful for you.

7. *Security:* It is important for your happiness that you are certain as to how things are going and your place in them.

8. *Recognition:* Doing things viewed as important by others is important for you.

9. *Adventure:* You desire change, a fast pace, and excitement in things you do.

10. *Freedom:* It is necessary for you to be free from constraints imposed by others.

11. *Materialism:* You enjoy amassing money or other assets.

12. *Religion:* It is important for you to adhere to a set of religious or moral principles.

Although you can probably think of a great number of other more specific needs, they could probably be included under one or another of these general categories. The need for social contact for example could be categorized under affiliation or altruism.

People have at least a vague idea about their needs, particularly in those situations where they have already had to act based on these needs. What most people have not done is undertake any kind of well-thought-out assessment of needs. This can help you to anticipate potential conflicts that may arise regarding your needs, and serve as a guide to those aspects of your life that usually call for some degree of planning.

It is difficult to do an assessment of your needs, especially within a book. But let us have a go at it, if for no other reason than to make you familiar with the process that is used.

To know more about your needs, you will find it useful to examine two areas: *what you have done and what you would like to do.* For those of you who are adults, your past behavior is the best indicator of your needs—"you are what you did it for." Your desires or preference for future behavior are important but make sure such desires are something more than a pipe dream.

One of the best ways to examine the needs evident in your past is to list important things you can remember about your life, things that you have done. These can be from any area of your life: work, school, recreation, childhood, to cite only a few. Examples might be winning an oratorical contest in grade six, establishing a sexual relationship with a person you found highly desirable, taking a dangerous canoe trip, giving birth, making money on the stock market, earning a promotion, passing a difficult course in college, getting the job you always wanted, or relaxing at a beach. The critical thing is that the incidents be important to you.

In the space below write down these important things you have done or experienced:

List I.   What Have You Done That Is Important to You?

1. _____
   _____

2. _____
   _____

3. _____
   _____

4. _____
   _____

5. _____
   _____

6. _____
   _____

7. _____
   _____

8. _____
   _____

9. _____
   _____

10. _____
    _____

11. _____
    _____

12. _____

Darryl was a forty-year-old high school English teacher. His list of important things included:

1. As senior committee member, Darryl designed a revised grade ten English curriculum. He then taught several workshops to his peers detailing the new program.

2. He won a race sailing event at the local level two years in a row.

3. While still in college, Darryl tutored a deaf student in reading skills. That student recently graduated from a top-notch technical institute.

4. He graduated in the top ten percent of his college class.

5. In elementary school Darryl was chosen to be class spokesperson during a dispute with a difficult teacher.

6. He successfully completed a course in home wine-making and won the novice event in the local wine-makers' competition.

7. He toured Europe with a friend on an essentials only budget.

8. Darryl shoplifted records as a teenager and was never caught.

9. In college he had two "serious love relationships"— both at the same time.

10. Darryl paid for a new house within twelve years of acquiring it.

11. He has stayed "successfully married" to the same woman for eighteen years.

12. Darryl's been asked to apply for assistant administrative positions on three occasions although he has refused each time.

As far as assessing your needs is concerned, the important thing is not the incident itself but your feelings about the incident. The behaviors you define as important may be illegal, immoral, or fattening—and they may still represent legitimate and important needs. The important question is: *Why is this incident important to you?*

Winning the grade six oratorical contest, for example, might be important because you beat the red-haired kid who sat in front of you or because it enabled you to join the academic clique or because others looked up to you or because of a combination of several reasons. Even though it is illegal, shoplifting records might be important because it gave you a sense of power or because it allowed you to be free from parental restrictions or because it allowed you to share your allowance with those who badly needed money.

Enjoying an experience is an indication that whatever you are doing is meeting a need. Since needs can be met in many ways, the important thing is not what you are doing but what you are doing it for.

For each incident you identified, try to identify one or several reasons why that incident is important to you. Write these possible reasons below.

List II.   Why Are These Incidents Important to You?

1. _____

   _____

2. _____

   _____

3. _____

   _____

4. _____

   _____

5. _____

   _____

6. _____

   _____

7. _____

   _____

8. _____

   _____

9. _____

   _____

10. _____

    _____

11. _____

    _____

12. _____

(This is not easy work and many people find it tedious. Remember that you do not have to consciously identify and isolate your needs in order to get a meaningful job. But it gives you valuable self-awareness that makes your search better focused and easier—so it is worth the trouble. It is especially valuable if you are at a loss as to where to go or if you are trying to identify a new career path.)

When Darryl looked over his list of important events, he found it difficult to identify precisely why many of the incidents were important to him. Often the reasons seemed conflicting. The reasons for each event are identified below.

1. Although he enjoyed writing the curriculum, Darryl enjoyed most the "basking in the limelight" after completion of the project. This was particularly evident when he taught the workshops to his peers.

2. For his sailing victories, he listed physical endurance and the recognition given to him in the local media as important.

3. Darryl had not thought much about this incident until quite recently when the deaf student had graduated, crediting Darryl with much of the early boost required to succeed. There was very little public recognition, but Darryl claimed that it gave him a "good feeling inside" to think about it.

4. Although being in the top ten percent of his college class was important, it was even more important that another individual, a rival during high school, did not make this grade.

5. His class spokesperson role was important because of the recognition it afforded. Years later he was still referred to as the "young ambassador."

6. Although he started winemaking on a whim, he enjoyed the activity. Winning the event was important because it proved that he could be successful in areas in which he was not trained.

7. On his European trip Darryl enjoyed the art galleries and museums as well as the social atmosphere of young people traveling together. He remembered the

informal competitions he would have with his friend to see who could survive the longest on the least money.

8. The excitement of doing something that others were afraid to do was very important at the time. Although Darryl had some regrets about stealing, it did alert him to strong needs that he felt—attention and competitiveness.

9. Darryl's duo romances were exciting, particularly since he had enjoyed a lackluster reputation in high school. Like the shoplifting, this event was important for what it showed Darryl that he needed.

10. It was important to Darryl that he not be beholden to anyone—and that everyone knew this to be the case. He held a big "mortgage burning party" to announce the event.

11. Darryl and his wife had had their ups and downs over the years, but it felt good to be still married when many of his friends were breaking up. Nowadays it seemed more important, more courageous to stay together than to break up.

12. Darryl was pleased to be asked to apply for the administration positions since it was an affirmation of his ability in the eyes of others. But he was afraid to accept because he did not like second-in-command positions and did not know how well he would do the job.

DREAMS AND ASPIRATIONS

The other information you can use to identify your needs are your dreams and aspirations—they are usually your accomplishments expressed in the future tense. Like your accomplishments, dreams tell a great deal about the needs you are seeking to fulfill in your daily life. It is not necessary that your dreams be realizable. It is necessary that you recognize why they are important for you. You may not be able to realize your dreams, but taking a close look at them makes it much more likely that you will meet your needs in one way or another.

Even though you may feel a little silly or embarrassed at first, try to identify some of your dreams or aspirations as a further step in specifying your needs. Forgetting about whether they seem possible or not, identify some things you would like to do, some things you would like to accomplish in the future:

List III.   Some Things You Would Like to Do

1. _____

_____

2. _____

_____

3. _____

_____

4. _____

_____

5. _____

_____

6. _____

_____

7. _____

   _____

8. _____

   _____

9. _____

   _____

10. _____

    _____

11. _____

    _____

12. _____

Like many of us, when Darryl tried to identify his wishes he had difficulty. It made him feel a little childish and he kept saying to himself, "Oh, I can't do that." However, eventually he produced the following.

1. Sail across the ocean single-handedly.

2. Be promoted to a principalship position without having to go through the assistant ranks.

3. Take a year off from teaching and live in another country.

4. Become an FM radio host specializing in literary broadcasting.

5. Adopt a child.

6. Build an expensive new home in the country.

7. Go back to school and earn a doctorate degree.

8. Have an affair.

Once again, as far as assessing your needs is concerned, the important thing is not the wish itself, but your feelings about the wish. The important question is: Why is this thing you would like to do important to you? There is no right answer, no reason that is more acceptable than another. Perhaps you want to quit your job and take up farming because you are afraid of competition, want the closeness of a small group, desire to help others, or because of a combination of several reasons.

For each wish you identified, try to identify one or several reasons why that wish is important to you. Write these possible reasons below:

List IV.   Why Are Your Wishes Important to You?

1. _____

   _____

2. _____

   _____

3. _____

   _____

4. _____

   _____

5. _____

   _____

6. _____

_____

7. _____

_____

8. _____

_____

9. _____

_____

10. _____

_____

11. _____

_____

12. _____

When Darryl analyzed why his wishes were important to him, he arrived at the following reasons.

1. He wanted to do something exciting, something that would prove to others that he could still "cut the mustard" and sailing alone did that.

2. As well as not having a principal to answer to, this promotion to principal would be good because it was

so seldom offered and only in recognition of superior talent.

3. Taking a year off appealed because it would feel good to just drop out, not have to answer to anybody or be anything.

4. He enjoyed artistic activity but seldom participated. Radio broadcasting would be a good way to start and would provide high public visibility.

5. Although childless by choice, he had begun to worry about his old age and other comforts of a family.

6. Darryl wanted something "very splashy" that would meet all his physical needs—and show others how far he had come. A country home would do that.

7. It was becoming increasingly difficult to progress without more training. Besides he always thought the title Dr. would be nice in front of his name.

8. Perhaps an affair is just a passing fancy, but Darryl had been thinking about it more and more in the past year.

In attempting to assess your needs, look carefully at List II and List IV. Do you see any common threads that seem to tie together your past behavior and your wishes? Some people find it useful to compare each of their past behaviors and wishes with the twelve needs outlined earlier. That may be a good place to start.

Without worrying about ordering your list in any way, write down a tentative list of needs that you have inferred from the exercise you have just completed.

List V.   Your Tentative List of Needs.

1. _____

_____

2. _____

_____

3. _____

_____

4. _____

_____

5. _____

_____

6. _____

_____

7. _____

_____

8. _____

_____

9. _____

_____

10 _____

_____

11. _____

_____

12. _____

If you have arrived at List V with something other than a blank piece of paper, you have come a long way. You may have identified needs such as a desire to be noticed by others, competing with others (at least when you win!), and helpfulness toward others. Obviously these tentative needs you have identified are not either-or situations; you may want at different times to be influential or one of the crowd, competitive or cooperative, require freedom or structure.

When Darryl looked over his lists of accomplishments and wishes he was uncertain as to which needs they reflected. His tentative list included:

1. Personal recognition. It was not sufficient that things be done well. They must be noticed.

2. Competitiveness. It felt good to beat somebody else even though Darryl felt that he "shouldn't feel that way."

3. Security. He could only feel happy if he felt in total control of his environment.

4. Excitement. Daring things were exciting but this often conflicted with security needs.

Sometimes spouses, friends, lovers, co-workers, or relatives can attempt to make us feel guilty, either directly or in a very subtle manner, because we do not exhibit a need that they deem to be important. Frequently, if we did demonstrate that need, it would be beneficial to them in some way—so they are far from impartial observers. In extreme cases, it is possible to live your whole life in such a way that you meet everybody else's needs except your own. Such people are seldom happy.

It is not easy to deal with others who would inflict on us their ideas of needs they think would be appropriate for us. It is sometimes helpful to change the conversation to why you are doing what you are doing—what needs you are trying to meet. Do not attempt to legitimize your needs to others. Present them as a given but remain open to the discussion of a particular behavior—if that behavior impacts on the other person in some way.

Needs are intensely personal and do not require justification from others. Most people demonstrate most needs to some degree.

Chapter 3

A Self-Assessment Questionnaire

"Well, you see, I am not, alas, the good simple fellow that
you suppose. Beneath this well-washed exterior there
beats a heart as black as a cockroach and fully half as
brave."—Mollo in *Shardik* by Richard Adams.

Other ways to identify and further refine your needs are to
ponder the personal preferences that reflect those needs. The
Self-Assessment Questionnaire outlines a number of personal
preferences or behaviors that are indicative of various needs. In
each case you are placed in a hypothetical situation and asked
to rate your satisfaction with a particular course of action.
There are no right answers to this questionnaire and although
your observations cannot be compared to a right answer or even
a norm, many people find personal insight in such an approach.

Listed below are four possible behaviors you can consider for
each of the twelve needs presented earlier. Think through each
one carefully, in terms of what you have enjoyed in the past or
might enjoy in the future. Do not worry about how competent
you might be at each activity. Let yourself go and focus on the
probable enjoyment that each proposed action might bring to
you.

By doing this exercise, you will be able to refine the tentative
needs (List V, p. 30) that you developed earlier. As you consider

the statements under each need, see how many of the statements you were able to agree with. Think through the implications of each one.

SELF-ASSESSMENT: IDENTIFYING YOUR NEEDS

1. Influence
(a) You would enjoy being asked for advice by others and find pleasure in providing such information.
(b) When policy is being planned for a group, you would prefer an active part in developing it.
(c) You would enjoy participating in heated discussions with others where you are able to put forward your beliefs and opinions.
(d) In a situation where a group of people have to do something, you enjoy the role of leader more than follower.

2. Altruism
(a) You would enjoy being part of worthy causes, of attempting to help others by your actions.
(b) You would contribute part of your earnings to charities in order to help others.
(c) You get upset with people who always seem to look out for number one.
(d) You worry about the underdog and would like to do what you can to help.

3. Affiliation
(a) You would feel more comfortable working on a task as part of a group rather than individually.
(b) You would tend to develop strong ties or feelings of loyalty for any organization you are part of.
(c) You would enjoy group activities rather than wholly individual pursuits.
(d) You are less excited by new things than you are about enjoying what you have.

4. Competition
(a) You would enjoy participating in competitive events, such as sports, games, contests, etc.

(b) You have difficulty accepting losing in events that have a win-lose dimension.

(c) You preform best in situations where you can gauge your progress against that of others.

(d) You like to be judged by results rather than by what you do to achieve those results.

5. Intellect

(a) You enjoy solving problems.

(b) You are more likely to enjoy planning how you would do something than going through the steps of doing it.

(c) You get less feeling of accomplishment from doing routine things where you already knew how to do them.

(d) You enjoy puzzles or games that are difficult, although you may tire of them quickly.

6. Aesthetics

(a) You get pleasure from viewing works of art or literature.

(b) You are able to express yourself by creating or making things that have little utilitarian value.

(c) You actively seek out artistic or literary encounters such as exhibitions, theater, etc.

(d) You are most satisfied when you work or play in an aesthetically pleasing environment.

7. Security

(a) You are most comfortable when you have established a routine.

(b) Even if things are going somewhat badly, you find it difficult to try something new.

(c) You prefer moderate, guaranteed long-term rewards to possible short-term rewards that may be greater.

(d) You are most productive when you feel safe and secure.

8. Recognition

(a) You enjoy "putting on a show" for others.

(b) You enjoy success most when others see your accomplishments.

(c) It is important for you that people with whom you are associated notice how well you do things.

(d) You might find yourself doing something you did not particularly enjoy so that others would comment favorably.

9. Adventure

(a) You tire of things quickly.
(b) You enjoy doing things that are risky just for the joy of doing them.
(c) You find that you must keep yourself revved up in order to be productive.
(d) The less things are the same day-after-day, the more you enjoy it.

10. Freedom

(a) It is important that you set your own rules.
(b) It is hard to be productive when somebody else tells you what to do, even if it is the same thing you would have done yourself.
(c) You are happiest when others make no demands on you.
(d) You find yourself wanting to "throw everything in" and start over, even when you are successful.

11. Materialism

(a) You would work mainly to obtain economic benefits.
(b) Success is gauged in terms of the bottom line as far as you are concerned.
(c) You enjoy making money, even when you do not need it for any particular purpose.
(d) It would be hard for you to be poor but happy.

12. Religion

(a) You find great meaning in the spiritual side of life.
(b) It is important to you that you actually practice your religion on a day-to-day basis.
(c) You find comfort in being able to relate your activities to a higher dimension.
(d) Religion is the one part of your life that keeps you going.

The behavior you enjoy is not your need. It is one way of expressing your need.

The more you focus on the various aspects of each need, the more information you will have to use in assessing the relative strength of your needs—which ones are more important than others.

To refine your list of tentative needs (List V, p. 30), complete the inventory below in terms of how important each need is to you. Use examples from your past (List I. p. 19) and intentions of your future (List III, p. 25) that support your decision for each need. Do not worry if your list is impractical or if it is not job related. It does not matter at this point.

List VI. Your Needs and Why?

1. Influence: _____

_____

_____

2. Altruism: _____

_____

_____

3. Affiliation: _____

_____

_____

4. Competition: _____

_____

_____

5. Intellect: _____

_____

_____

6. Aesthetics: _____

_____

_____

7. Security: _____

_____

_____

8. Recognition: _____

_____

_____

9. Adventure: _____

_____

_____

10. Freedom: _____

_____

_____

11. Materialism: _____

_____

_____

12.   Religion: _____

_____

_____

In attempting to clarify your needs, do not worry about being hemmed-in, about feeling that you have to state them in black-white terms. Your needs probably include a few that are easily identified as important but also a number of others that are less clearly defined. You may even feel that none of your needs are definite—everything is more-or-less tentative. Do not panic— you cannot be more certain than you are. In this assessment you are trying to ignore *shoulds* and tell it like it is. Remember that in the long term it is the *process* of needs identification that is the most important. It is this process you can use at many points in your life to sort out where you are or where you would like to be.

Chapter 4

Meeting Your Needs

"We need some imaginative stimulus, some not impossible ideal such as may shape vague hope, and transform it into effective desire, to carry us year after year, without disgust, through the routine-work which is so large a part of life."—*Marius the Epicurean* by Walter Pater

I said before that the two critical questions surrounding your needs and your career are: "What are your needs?" and "How will you choose to act them out?" Now that you have explored the first of these, the time has come to deal with the second—what you do about what you have discovered.

As significant as your needs are to your life, it is not likely that every one of them can be satisfied or met through your work or any other single pursuit. Nor is it likely that every unmet need will be fully realizable in any given time period in your life. Determining your priorities and compromise are your most effective tools. You will always have unmet needs and there will always be work and non-work opportunities to meet those needs.

Life is full of opportunities and a good part of it is accidental. Every day a variety of situations—opportunities—are presented to you that you can either take advantage of or ignore. The kind of response you make depends not only on your needs, but also how you understand these needs and how you are acting out these needs at present.

> Arlice was a department manager in a large city branch of a national department store. Although she enjoyed administration, she was not happy about living in the city.
>
> Using her informal contacts within the company, Arlice learned that there would soon be a position in management out West in a new store that was about to open. Although it was usual company policy to hire locally and train junior management staff, Arlice was able to persuade her company to allow a transfer—and to a more senior position. The position would never have been advertised internally.

Although a job or a career provides you with a rich opportunity to meet some of your needs, it is not the only opportunity to do so.

To retain your sanity it is important that, as you combine the various elements of your life, you make sure that there is a general fulfillment of your needs. Even though some needs may go unmet, you will generally be more satisfied if most of them can be accounted for in one way or another.

Career planning is life planning in miniature. It is nothing less than determining which of your needs (and to what extent) you will seek to meet through work. (You're right. It sounds easier than it is.)

YOUR PRESENT SITUATION

If you have completed List VI (p. 37), you have probably got a good idea of what your most important needs are as well as some supporting documentation for why they matter. That is a good place to start in assessing which of your needs are being met through your work, which through other aspects of your life, and which are going unmet.

In doing career planning you are really looking for gaps—gaps between your needs and what you are currently doing to meet those needs. Once you have located those gaps, you can choose to do something to fill them.

How do you identify the gaps? You will need to construct another list. This time you will be attempting to discover if your important needs are being met in your present life circumstances. Here's how it's done.

1. Select one of your needs from List VI (p. 37). Write it in the blank in List VII (p. 42).

2. In the space labeled *Work,* write down what you are currently doing in your employment to meet that need. Obviously if you are not working, leave this space blank.

3. In the space labeled *Other,* write down what you are doing in other aspects of your life (hobbies, family, volunteer, etc.) to meet that need.

4. In the space labeled *Satisfaction,* indicate whether or not you feel that this need is being satisfied by your work and nonwork activities. Is the need fully met, met hardly at all, or is there just a small imbalance between the strength of your need and your level of satisfaction? Do not worry about how you would make yourself more satisfied, or even if this satisfaction would come from work or nonwork activities. For now just focus on the amount of your satisfaction.

5. Repeat steps 1 through 4 for as many needs as you choose.

List VII.   Your Needs Analysis

1. Need: _____

   Work: _____

   _____

Other: _____

_____

_____

Satisfaction: _____

_____

_____

2. Need: _____

   Work: _____

   _____

   Other: _____

   _____

   _____

   Satisfaction: _____

   _____

   _____

3. Need: _____

   Work: _____

   _____

Other: _____

_____

_____

Satisfaction: _____

_____

_____

4. Need: _____

Work: _____

_____

Other: _____

_____

_____

Satisfaction: _____

_____

_____

5. Need: _____

Work: _____

_____

Other: _____

_____

_____

Satisfaction: _____

_____

_____

6. Need: _____

Work: _____

_____

Other: _____

_____

_____

Satisfaction: _____

_____

_____

PUTTING IT ALL TOGETHER

To repeat what I said earlier, it is important for the quality of your life that you achieve a general meeting of your needs, especially if you want to avoid the kind of crisis that will require you to pay someone like me outrageous amounts of money to help when you ignore your needs. With List VII (p. 42) you now have the basic information required for sound career decisions.

Now that you have identified the gaps between your needs and what you are currently doing to meet those needs, what should you do to cope with these gaps? How do you get from where you are to where you want to be? The gaps exist either because you do not have enough behaviors to satisfy one of your needs or you have behaviors that conflict with a need. You can be damned if you do or damned if you don't.

To illustrate the point, I will deal with these gaps only from the perspective of career planning. The same process could be used for other areas of your life, but you will have to make that application yourself.

From the perspective of your career the two types of gaps translate into two types of questions.

1. What are you doing in your current work situation that could cause a potential needs conflict?
    —Are these behaviors voluntary?
    —Are they central to your job?
    —What scope is there for change?
    —How strong are the needs, the conflict, and your motivation to change things?
    —What alternatives are available to you?

2. Which of your needs requiring additional satisfaction could potentially be met through work?
    —Can you meet these needs in your present job? How?
    —What alternatives are there to meeting these needs through work?
    —How strong are these needs and what will happen if you do nothing?
    —How much effort are you prepared to put into meeting these needs?
    —What alternatives are available to you?

NEEDS CONFLICTS

Whether you are currently working or looking for a job, the question of conflicts is still important since it could pertain to a job you have or might secure. There is a temptation to look at possible jobs much more in terms of their positive elements, what needs they can satisfy, rather than in terms of what compromises might have to be made. The important thing is that the compromises be made rationally, with the trade-offs clear in your own mind.

Greg was a successful salesman at a prospering new car dealership, a dealership characterized by a hard-sell, close-at-all-costs philosophy on the part of most salesmen.

Although he enjoyed selling cars, Greg never felt quite comfortable with what he thought were manipulative selling techniques. "I just don't think you have to do it that way. But everybody else does," he lamented.

In a CareerScan workshop Greg was encouraged to rethink his basic assumptions regarding the necessity of using the sales approach he was so uncomfortable with. He also received coaching in sales techniques that were more in line with his own philosophy and orientation. Today he is still a successful salesman but a lot happier in what he is doing.

Problems with needs conflicts are potentially more dangerous than those stemming from lack of adequate satisfaction. After all, if you are unsatisfied on the job, you have various other areas (home, hobbies, work, etc.) to obtain satisfaction from. However, a needs conflict in the work area requires direct action, that cannot come from another area of your life. You have little choice; change your need (easier said than done) or change your work (but not necessarily the job).

Changing your work can range from dropping voluntary behaviors that interfere with a need (Greg's original selling techniques) to a complete job change that is more in line with your needs (moving from sales to foreign missionary work). Where you fit on this continuum depends on your answers to the first set of questions.

Sharon, age thirty-four, had been working at home for the past eight years after resigning her accountant's position to raise a family. She was becoming increasingly dissatisfied with her situation.

"I'm just not happy working at home anymore," she said. "All the things I'm doing don't seem to be important."

An assessment indicated that Sharon had several unmet needs in her present work situation. She had a high need to be in contact with others, was highly money oriented, and required intellectual stimulation.

Several possible ways to satisfy these unmet needs were explored—volunteering, part-time and full-time work.

It soon became evident to Sharon that, given the degree of her needs, they were unlikely to be met without returning to her previous career in accounting. She still faced a dilemma since she couldn't stay at home with her family and work. However, she had clarified her choices, and the awareness that she would continue to have unmet needs until she changed her situation made her decision less difficult.

How to Deal With Needs Conflicts in the Workplace

1. Be certain that the problem is not merely in your perception of the situation. What requires you to behave the way that you deem to be unacceptable? Does such behavioral expectation result from managerial edict, custom, or is

"everybody doing it"? If possible, identify individuals who are not behaving in the prescribed manner—and the effects of such noncompliance.

2. If the problem is mainly in your perception of the situation or the behaviors you deem to be unacceptable are not required, identify how you can change what you are doing. Remember that it is usually easier to substitute another behavior for the one you find troublesome than it is to simply stop the behavior. If necessary, get professional help at this stage. (See p. 88 for how to select professional help.)

3. If your problem is not completely in your perception of the situation, specifically identify which behaviors are in conflict with your needs. Identify what might be done to deal with these conflicts (transfer, reassignment, etc.). Speak candidly with a trusted co-worker or supervisor to identify the possibility of change within your present position or of other opportunities within the company. Be careful to identify the conflicting requirements as your problem, not as what ought or ought not to be done by the company. Do not be sanctimonious.

4. If you are unable to resolve your needs' conflict and if the issue is a major one as far as you are concerned, the only alternative may be to leave your present employment. Armed with the awareness of your needs, be careful that the new positions you consider are more in line with your needs.

SATISFYING YOUR NEEDS

Increasing your needs' satisfaction is a major part of long-term career aspirations. The answers you give to the following questions can help you focus on how you will search for job satisfaction.

Remember that work is not a magical place to meet your needs. However, since a full-time job occupies so much of your time, you will undoubtedly find that job more meaningful if at least some of your needs are met through your work. But which ones?

A job is not the only place you can meet your needs, but it is a major opportunity to do so.

Several years ago when General Motors was expanding plant operations, they were seeking a janitorial staff. They opened these positions to current employees first, expecting that a few burnt-out workers near retirement age might be interested. Unexpectedly they received hundreds of applications from a broad cross section of employees, some young and successful in their current positions.

For most people economy of time dictates that as well as not violating strong needs, their work must provide a positive atmosphere for exercising personal needs. Work must be meaningful in meeting some of your needs for you to be successful at it. Of course, you could satisfy a strongly felt need for competition in after-work sports activity but you would probably be that much more satisfied if your work allowed for this expression as well.

The dichotomy of meeting none of your needs through work and relying totally on extra-work time for satisfaction can be schizophrenic.

To become more satisfied, it is important that you decide how you will meet the gaps between your needs and your behavior. Let us look at a sequential flow chart you can use in order to do that.

1. Identify the needs that are currently not being met in your life. Refer to List VII (page 47).
2. Separate these unmet needs into three categories.
    (a) Those that must be met through work that could be accommodated in your current job.

_____

_____

_____

(b) Those that must be met through work that cannot be accommodated in your current job.

_____

_____

_____

(c) Those that can be accommodated through nonwork activity.

_____

_____

_____

3. If you are currently working, identify what you could do in your present job that would enable you better to meet these needs. Identify the feasibility of doing these things within the confines of your present position or other positions within your organization.

Deal with needs categorized as 2a in the same manner as you would have dealt with needs conflicts on the job. Decide how much scope there is within your present position. If possible, expand that scope by discussion with your employer.

4. If you have needs that must be met through work that cannot be accommodated in your current job you are in the same position as if you had an unresolvable needs conflict in your present job. Resolution may come only in a job change. Job change requires consideration of far more than your needs. Refer to Sections II and III of *CareerScan*.

Be wary that you do not underestimate the latitude of your present job—or present employer. One of the characteristic errors made by people who are evaluating their life circumstances is the "baby and the bathwater" syndrome.

Because your present situation is imperfect, because you have articulated your unmet needs, you may have a wish to make a clean break, to start fresh. Unfortunately, there are seldom any truly fresh starts and, whenever possible, you are better off trying to remake your present circumstances.

5. Investigate nonwork avenues you could use to meet the needs identified as 2c. Perhaps volunteering, a hobby, church activity, or just plain lazing around would help. Whatever your choice, be aware that this may involve reducing the amount of time or resources you will have for fulfillment of work-related needs.

You will be happiest when you meet your needs. You will be wise when you recognize the many opportunities to do so.

SELECTING A SPECIFIC JOB THAT MEETS YOUR NEEDS

If you are not working at present but want to meet some of your needs through work or if you have decided that your present job cannot satisfy the needs you want to meet through work, you are probably job hunting. You are looking for a job that will meet your needs. But where to begin?

First, although I have been talking almost exclusively about your needs in Section I, do not forget that there are other important things to consider in the job selection process—your abilities and the demands of the job. These two areas are discussed in Section II of *CareerScan*.

Second, along with deciding which of your needs you will seek to meet through work, it is a good idea to gather information that will help you decide if a specific job is likely to meet your needs. There are several ways to do just that.

A job, any job, is a compromise.

One way to establish the likelihood of a job meeting your needs is to look carefully at individuals already working at that job. Try to establish what it is they get out of their job. Although you probably will not get exactly the same thing out of a job as someone else, observing several people can provide you a good idea of the possible range of needs that could be satisfied by any given job.

You will have to use your imagination in order to meet people working at the type of job you are considering. It is not as difficult as you might imagine. One of the best ploys is to telephone someone, tell them that you are considering a career in their area, and ask to talk to them (perhaps over lunch) to get a better idea of the job. Most people will be flattered that you have selected them as representative of their industry and after the first few awkward moments will usually be very candid in discussing their job. As a side benefit, you will be establishing contacts that you can use later when you are actively searching for a job.

If you are too busy or too shy to use this direct technique, consider enrolling in seminars, courses, or attending professional meetings that pertain to the job you are considering.

In discussing a job keep in mind that the person you select may not have consciously identified which of their needs the job meets. You will probably have to do that for yourself based on their responses to questions about the scope of their job, which parts of their job they find satisfying and why, as well as about less positive dimensions of the work.

Another way to discover the needs that a specific job will meet for you is to learn as much about the job as you can and identify concretely how that job will meet the needs you have singled out as important. Take each need that you have identified as important and ask yourself what will you be doing on a job that will assist you to meet that need? If you cannot specifically identify what you will be doing that will meet those needs, be wary of opting for that job.

It is usual to find, on close examination, that any job you are considering meets some of your needs, does not meet others, and may be in violation of still others. That is where trade-offs come into play. Perhaps a need you wanted to meet through work can be met in another way. Perhaps the violation is small enough that you can disregard it. Perhaps that job is not as promising as you first thought. At the very least, you now have a system to analyze the opportunities that are available to you in terms of the needs you have.

Do not expect any job to be a perfect match for your needs. But don't ignore your needs if they cannot be met through your work.

WHY YOU AVOID CAREER DECISIONS

There are two factors that stand in the way of many people making conscious career decisions: the first is fear; the second is perfectionism.

Fear is the greatest crippler because it frequently operates unconsciously, showing itself in a wide range of capricious ways. The classic fear of decision-making is also the fear of career decision-making—the fear of making a mistake. The fear of risking a mistake can cause you to postpone decisions, "I'll do it tomorrow," or to endlessly seek advice (and thus decisions) from others: "I'll let my counselor (psychiatrist, boss, friend, lover) decide."

Such behavior does not free you from the *results* of poor decisions. What it does is give you the illusion that you are not accountable for the results. Whether you end up sitting on top of the world or in the blackest hole, all you can honestly say is, "It wasn't my fault. I didn't make the decision." While you have purchased the hollow guarantee that you are not responsible for your own failures you have just about guaranteed that you will have no successes.

Paul was thirty-eight-years-old and still kidded that he had not yet decided what he wanted to do when he grew up. Finishing a general arts degree when he was twenty-one, Paul had drifted into advertising because his father had told him it was a good road to the top.

Seventeen years later Paul was still in advertising—at least his body was. While moderately successful in his field, he often felt that he was being pushed and pulled in every direction by others. At the same time he was reluctant to make decisions himself for fear of making a mistake.

Paul was stuck—and miserable.

In career decision-making if fear does not get you, perfectionism will! You fall victim when you start believing that out there someplace exists the perfect job for you. It is up to you to find it. This same reasoning has spawned searches for the perfect lover, the flawless apartment, the ideal exercise or diet plan, and the holy grail. Generally it is a search that has produced a great deal more heat than light.

There is no perfect job for you. There is no perfect career for you. There are probably a number of good fits, but rarely is there anything that comes even close to perfection. By and large, jobs are static, at least on a day-by-day basis. They do not reliably provide you with one type of satisfaction on one day and another on the next. By contrast you are dynamic. What you need and require in your life, and particularly from your job, changes on a day-by-day basis. If we compare your requirements and what is available to meet those requirements from your work, there will always be a gap. If you are not prepared to decide until that gap is zero, you will not decide.

Laurie was twenty-nine-years-old, a junior laywer employed for the last six months by an international oil company. During the five years since her graduation from law school, she had held four different jobs. Each one had been approached full of promise but was quickly discarded. In one case the salary was too low; another was too far from her home; yet another required extensive weekend work.

"Something always seems to be wrong with whatever I choose," she lamented during an interview. "They are never just what I want and something better always seems to come along."

Regrettably Laurie's career success was as limited as her tenure at any one company. Now at twenty-nine, she was supervised by a younger lawyer and was thinking of quitting. "I've decided I want a job with more responsibility," she told her boss. "Something that's more in line with what I can do."

It does not follow that because there is no perfect job for you any job or no job will do. That is just another form of opting out, of deciding by not deciding. A job or a coherent collection of jobs (career) can be chosen for a variety of reasons, perhaps to fulfill some inner needs or drives, perhaps to give you enough free time to fulfill those needs elsewhere. There is no right reason for choosing or refusing a job. When you choose for yourself rather than doing nothing and letting circumstances choose for you, you have a much greater chance of deeper and more varied satisfactions.

SECTION I: SUMMARY

1. You do not need a life goal. Careers are largely the result of making or responding to opportunity.

2. Needs are important and it is important that you understand your needs.

3. Enjoying something is an indicator that you are meeting your needs. What you are enjoying is not the need.

4. There are many ways, work and nonwork, to meet your needs.

5. Work *can* provide a major opportunity to meet your needs but it does not necessarily do so.

6. Logical life planning is deciding how you will meet your needs. Logical career management is deciding which of your needs, and to what degree, you will seek to fulfill through work.

SECTION II

Selecting a Job

"Work thou for pleasure—paint, or sing, or carve
The thing thou lovest, though the body starve—
Who works for glory misses oft the goal;
Who works for money coins his very soul.
Work for the work's sake, then, and it may be
That these things shall be added unto thee."
—*Work* by Kenyon Cox

— you want to get a better idea of your own abilities—and how these rate in terms of the demands of the marketplace.
— you have difficulty in translating your needs into a specific job or career.
— you need some method to evaluate jobs: what they can give you and what they will demand of you.
— you need to make a job decision in the near future and want to minimize the risk such a decision entails.
— you have completed Section I and wonder, "What's next?"
— you have worked in some field and have accrued some successes—and failures.

— you know what kind of job you are after and want to get on with getting it.
— you are not prepared to make hard decisions and compromises about what you want.
— you already know your strengths and weaknesses.
— you already have a good idea about the abilities employers are looking for.

Chapter 5

Opportunities

"When the sunne shineth, make hay.
When the iron is hot, strike.
And while I at length debate and beate the bush,
There shall steppe in other men and catch the burdes."
—*Proverbs* by John Heywood

The choice of a job is one of the most important decisions you will make in your lifetime. Probably only the choice of a spouse ranks in the same league. Granted with jobs the choice can and usually will be repeated again and again throughout your life, but each decision will pass your way only once.

I said in Section I that you do not need a life goal to make viable career choices. I should have been more emphatic. A life goal seldom helps in job selection and may actually hinder your chances for real job satisfaction or career happiness. Such things as establishing a life goal to reach a certain career-position or salary by a certain age may hinder you because it can cause you to rate your present opportunities in terms of some ultimate rainbow rather than in terms of what is available today.

The problem with life goals comes when, having sacrificed your shorter term aspirations along the way, you are not happy even if you do achieve them.

Darlene has held several important but seemingly unrelated positions over the past fifteen years. She has been a home economics teacher, full-time mother, radio host, free-lance writer, consultant, and educational coordinator. She handled each job superbly.

Darlene is often amazed when opportunities come along and even more amazed that she is selected to fill them. "Each time, I try for the job because it is something I want to do. It offers me a challenge and the chance to do something different," she says. Employers eagerly select her for jobs because she truly seems to want the positions—and because she is developing a reputation for doing anything she does very well.

"It's easy to do well when you're doing what you want to do. It's almost like working for yourself," Darlene indicated in interview. "I know I won't be happy here in a few years, but by then something else will come along," she says optimistically.

Career success is not something to be strived for directly. It is the natural by-product of meeting your needs and maximizing the opportunities that come your way.

RECOGNIZING AND CREATING OPPORTUNITIES

Since opportunities rather than life goals are the most important as far as career planning is concerned, it is critical that you be able to recognize opportunities when they come your way. It is equally important you realize the part you have to play in creating your own opportunities.

A dictionary definition of opportunity relates it to a favorable juncture of circumstances, something you feel would result in a positive outcome for you. Defined in terms of career or work, an opportunity is a possible work situation that could lead to the meeting of some of your needs.

Unfortunately many people view a work opportunity simply in terms of possible job advancement to positions of greater authority or responsibility—whether or not such advancement meets their needs. This is a mistake because it lets either someone else or societal pressure define the need and how it should be met. Situations such as this account for the unhappiness of many middle executives who have progressed to their current positions by a combination of their own talent and someone else's idea of what should make them happy.

Knowledge of your needs gives you a basis on which to assess any opportunity you are aware of. What is an opportunity for somebody else could be a disaster for you—or vice versa. Satisfaction of needs is a very individual matter.

Opportunities for meeting your needs through work confront you every day. This is particularly true once you free yourself from the millstone of life goals. Let us look at some ways to recognize—or create—opportunities.

1. Make certain you understand your needs, as well as which needs are unfulfilled in your present life circumstances.

2. In evaluating any opportunity that is thrust upon you, such as a promotion, transfer, or enlarged responsibility, always evaluate the needs this new position will satisfy for you. Also look carefully at what compromises might have to be made in terms of needs your present position meets that your new position may not meet. Do not allow others to define your opportunities for you.

3. A rich place to look for opportunities is in the problems that confront you or your employer. Whether the problem is in poor paperflow, delinquent accounts receivable, faulty internal communication, or lagging sales, try to devise solutions that meet your needs. Addressing such problems with your proposed solutions before you are asked to implement someone else's solution will increase the likelihood that you will be able to meet your needs.

4. Since needs are only met through work if you are at least minimally competent at whatever you do, ensure that your technical and nontechnical skills are honed to a degree that will allow you to succeed. Opportunities are always

greatest for those who have demonstrated competence at whatever they are already doing.

5. If you find yourself losing interest in your job, look for changes in your needs as well as the ability of your present job to meet those needs.

6. Share your aspirations with those who have the power to change things. Keeping your boss informed about what you want to get out of work improves the chances that you will be able to do so. A good time for this is during your regular performance appraisal session.

7. Evaluate a variety of positions within your company to decide in advance what needs they might satisfy for you. Map your proposed career in terms of this evaluation rather than in terms of a life goal.

8. If possible, always have an alternate plan for meeting your needs, both by work and nonwork activities, should your first choice not prove possible.

Jack is a well-respected senior professor at a large Midwestern college. Although he has been offered a prestigious department head position on three occasions, he has always declined.

"It's not what I want to do," he says, "but nobody seems to understand how I could turn it down. I mean, it's more money, less teaching, and a good deal more authority, but I don't think I'd like it."

Jack had analyzed what he needs from his job and was quite right in asserting that a promotion would be a mistake.

Most people do not recognize their opportunities because they do not understand their needs.

AFTER NEEDS—WHAT THEN?

If you have arrived at this point, you should already have a pretty good idea of your needs—and which ones you will seek to fulfill through some form of work. You may not know where you are going, but you do know what you are looking for. To be successful in this search, you will have to consider what a job will demand and what you have to offer.

Chapter 6

Abilities + Action = Accomplishments

"I love to watch the rooster crow,
He's like so many men I know
Who brag and bluster, rant and shout
And beat their manly breasts
without
The first damn thing to crow
about."—*The Rooster* by John Kendrick Bangs

YOU AND YOUR ABILITIES

You select a job for your own selfish reasons—your needs. You are selected for a job for somebody else's selfish reasons—what has to be done and how well somebody thinks you will be able to do it.

To get the job you want, you will have to put your needs aside for the time being and focus on what you have to offer a prospective employer—your abilities. What you have to offer an employer is what may get you the opportunity to meet your needs through work.

For the sake of simplicity let us divide your attributes into two major areas: technical and nontechnical. Technical abilities are skills, usually obtained by specific training or experience, that enable you to perform certain job-related activities.

Knowledge of how to program a computer using COBOL, skill in the mechanics of running an employee recruiting campaign, ability to use insurance actuarial tables, facility in performing statistical analysis—all are examples of technical abilities. Technical abilities are identifiable primarily because they are observable and involve action. Usually, there are generally accepted standards for success in technical skill areas. In fact, it may be just as important to know how you obtained your technical skills (accreditation) as it is that you have them.

Nontechnical skills are those abilities that enable you to function more effectively. They are usually learned, although they are seldom formally taught. Most people who are highly skilled in this area seem to have acquired their skills "naturally." A skill such as interpersonal effectiveness is included here, as are other nebulous factors, including learning ability, planning skills, and knowledge of sales techniques.

Nontechnical skills are difficult to define and measure because they must be inferred from what you do. Whereas technical skills vary greatly from one occupation to another, nontechnical skills cut across occupations. You might say that nontechnical skills are the grease that allows the bearing (technical skills) to perform well.

Although you may presume that you will get a job on the basis of your technical qualifications, most people, including most recruiters, overemphasize the importance of such abilities as they relate to job success. Technical skills set the basic requirements for the job you want; nontechnical skills determine your success beyond a basic level. As well, jobs vary greatly in their ratio of technical to nontechnical skills. Some jobs do not have any readily identifiable technical skills, while all jobs require a variety of nontechnical ones.

In a ten-year study conducted by the author with technical professionals (engineers, geologists, etc.) most of their demonstrated career success was attributable to nontechnical interpersonal factors. Technical abilities were necessary but far from sufficient for career success. Most people in the study were technically competent, or perhaps more correctly, technically similar.

Technical skills are often what get you your job—nontechnical skills determine how successful you will be at it.

Peter was the successful CEO of an international mining corporation. Although trained as an engineer, he was, by his own admission, only modestly talented in engineering. Yet over a twenty-year period spanning five companies, he had rapidly progressed to the top.

If you asked those who worked for him from the VPs to the hard-rock miners why Peter was successful, they all said the same thing—"He knows how to get things done."

It was true. If you took a hard look at Peter and what he did, he did know how to "get things done." He fit in well with everybody, seemed to know just when to say what, and kept everything moving along smoothly. And, aside from a few aspects, Peter's job as head of a technical corporation required few technical skills.

ASSESSING YOUR TECHNICAL ABILITIES

The most valid way to assess your technical abilities—the way a prospective employer will—is to assess what you have done. Anything other than performance is a maybe and a poor second best. Raw potential is important when you first graduate from college: at such times an employer has nothing better on which to base a decision. Even in cases where the new position differs from your last job, an employer looks at your past performance in order to infer your potential for the new job.

Your skills and abilities are defined by inference on the part of others. The inference they make will be governed in large part by what they see in your past.

I once conducted a seminar for personal recruiters employed by small and large North American firms. A major aspect of this seminar focused on establishing the criteria for employee selection. Although there was a good deal of difference between what each of the recruiters looked for in prospective candidates, they were virtually unanimous on how they actually looked.

"I look to see what they've done. I figure, if they ain't done, they ain't gonna do," was the way one recruiter put it.

You cannot change what you have done in the past but you can seek to understand it. If you do that, you are already two steps ahead of most job seekers—or employers—for two reasons. First, it allows you to get a good handle on your own abilities which in turn helps you make realistic job choices. Second, it provides you with the information you will need to sell yourself to a prospective employer (more about this in Section III).

Realistic job choices should be based on what you need in the job as well as your skills or ability to handle the job. You may find a job that meets all of your needs to be one that you do not have the technical or nontechnical skills to perform well. Conversely, a prospective job may be too routine for your level of ability. In either case, you are unlikely to be able to meet your needs.

Diana was a senior staff recruiter for a multinational oil company. She had risen through the ranks quickly, each time opting for jobs she thought she would enjoy.

Although her job as recruiter was satisfying in many ways, Diana wanted a position with more status and responsibility. When a position of Manager, Employee Planning, became vacant, she went all out to get it.

She was successful in obtaining her new job, but Diana quickly became dissatisfied with it. The position required a great deal of statistical analysis and reporting, two areas in which she performed poorly.

Although she had sought the position for its status and responsibility, Diana felt she was getting little needs satisfaction from it. She felt more uncomfortable than ever before and had to constantly put herself on guard against making costly mistakes. She hated the thought of going backward in her career but felt she had little choice. Eventually she applied for her old job with another employer and was much happier.

You will not achieve satisfaction of your needs in jobs that you cannot do well. Choosing a job because of what it can give you, without considering what you can give the job, is a mistake. Luckily such mistakes are seldom irreversible and you can often learn as much or more from them as you can from correct choices.

Career success involves striking a balance between finding a job that meets your needs and one at which you have the skills to be successful.

There are several ways to assess your abilities, only a few of which are possible within the pages of *CareerScan*. The most valid way is to do what a prospective employer might do—analyze your past accomplishments. Here is how to do it.

STEP 1. IDENTIFY YOUR ACCOMPLISHMENTS

Accomplishments, for purposes of this exercise, are tasks you have done well that others would consider important. They may be different from those things in Section I of CareerScan you identified as being important to you, because, although these are achievements you feel highlight your abilities, they must also be something that others would judge as significant because they involve at least a modest degree of initiative or ability.

Accomplishments may come from work activity (that is best) or nonwork activity. Examples may be putting together a major report, firing an obnoxious employee, coordinating a difficult staff meeting, balancing a precarious family budget, or planning a conference.

Many people have trouble identifying accomplishments because they say, "Oh, that wasn't important. It was just part of my job." They have done a thing so frequently, and often so well, they feel that it does not take any special ability. It is those very things that you should be identifying as accomplishments. Very few of us (including the author) have won a Nobel prize. All of us have something to crow about.

At this point write your accomplishments on the list below. Do not worry about how they are phrased since they need only remind you of what you have done.

List VIII.   Your Accomplishments

1. _____

_____

_____

2. _____

_____

_____

3. _____

_____

_____

Abilities + Action = Accomplishments

4. _____

_____

_____

5. _____

_____

_____

6. _____

_____

_____

7. _____

_____

_____

8. _____

_____

_____

9. _____

_____

_____

10. _____

_____

_____

During a career development seminar, Glen, a forty-year-old controller of a Fortune 500 company, produced the following list when asked to identify his accomplishments.

1. Designed a computerized financial reporting system used by three subsidiary companies.

2. Worked closely with outside consultants to justify the use of microcomputers within the company.

3. Was able to better regulate inventory, thus reducing short-term interest charges incurred by the company.

4. Was asked by a local university to teach financial class for graduate students. Was very successful at doing so.

5. Fostered an "executives in training" program within the company, thus ensuring a supply of long-term talent.

6. Participated in a grueling physical challenge program for executives involving mountain climbing, backpacking, and wilderness survival.

7. Codeveloped and implemented an innovative performance appraisal system for executive level personnel within his division.

8. Developed and implemented the strategy for taking over the operation of a competitor.

9. Wrote two articles for financial publications; one involved a great deal of technical information.

Jane was an experienced teacher who had spent the past five years at home raising a young family. She wanted to reenter teaching and composed the following list of accomplishments during a career reentry seminar.

1. Set up an enrichment program for gifted children while teaching elementary school.

2. Graduated near the top of class in undergraduate university teacher training. Program was experimental and focused on individualizing student instruction.

3. Taught elementary school at a large inner-city school. Developed a novel extra-mural physical education program for these students.

4. Instructed a time management seminar for other teachers at the request of the regional teachers' association.

5. Completed three classes toward a Master's degree in Education by part-time study.

6. Evaluated a new reading program for her teaching district.

7. Had one article dealing with creative language activities for young children accepted for publication in a national teaching magazine.

In job selection your accomplishments are important not for what they mean to you but for what others will infer about you from them.

STEP 2. TRANSLATE YOUR ACCOMPLISHMENTS INTO TECHNICAL SKILLS

Once you have identified a selection of your accomplishments, the important thing to focus on is not the accomplishment per se but the technical skills that they required. Try not to be too general in labeling your skill; each accomplishment may require several skills.

The technical skills required in writing a major geological report may include knowledge of geological formations, ability to use statistical computer software, ability to interpret complex geophysical data, as well as the components of technical report writing.

73

List IX.   Your Technical Skills

For each accomplishment you identified in Step 1, write down the technical skills that were necessary to do the job. At this point do not worry about nontechnical skills such as interpersonal ability or verbal persuasiveness.

1. _____

_____

_____

2. _____

_____

_____

3. _____

_____

_____

4. _____

_____

_____

5. _____

_____

_____

Abilities + Action = Accomplishments

6. _____

_____

_____

7. _____

_____

_____

8. _____

_____

_____

9. _____

_____

_____

10. _____

_____

_____

Glen had some difficulty in isolating the technical skills from indefinable nontechnical skills in deciding what was important to realize his accomplishments. He produced the following list "very tentatively."

1. Knowledge of financial modeling systems. Knowledge of computer hardware and financial planning software.

2. Knowledge of strengths and limitations of microcomputers. Knowledge of computing requirements of large organizations. Cost effectiveness computing abilities.

3. Familiarity with inventory recording and reporting systems. Detailed knowledge of user requirements. Ability to interface computer systems with noncomputer staff.

4. General knowledge of financial theory. Teaching skills.

5. Knowledge of staff requirements for large organization. Selling ability.

6. Physical stamina. Survival techniques.

7. Knowledge of performance appraisal systems. Knowledge of legalities concerning performance systems.

8. Detailed financial analysis knowledge. Stock and securities knowledge. Knowledge of banking, borrowing, and anti-trust legislation.

9. Technical writing skills. General financial theory knowledge.

Jane listed the following skills as indicative of the accomplishments she had identified.

1. Knowledge of theory of gifted children. Program design abilities.

2. Rapid learning abilities and persistence. Specialized knowledge of individualized curriculum.

3. Initiative and knowledge of physical education principles. Organizational abilities.

4. Effective instructional techniques. Time management.

5. Educational administration. Persistence.

6. Writing skills, time organization. Creativity.

If you can identify your accomplishments, you will be able to verify your skills to others.

NONTECHNICAL SKILLS

Except for work requiring highly specialized knowledge exercised in a hermitlike atmosphere, there is almost no accomplishment that can be realized using only technical skills. Nontechnical skills are the catalyst that allows technical acumen to function effectively. It is one thing to know how to complete a client's detailed business taxation forms and quite another to communicate effectively with the client in order to obtain the required information.

The range of nontechnical skills is broad and the labels applied to such skills are often confusing. What one person calls communications skills another person might call interpersonal effectiveness. As well, many of the nontechnical skills are not really skills at all—they are really more properly called personal characteristics.

Measurement of competence in nontechnical skills is also difficult so that it is hard to assess if an individual is competent in a specific skill or if that skill is required for a certain job.

Generally speaking nontechnical skills include those that are concerned with how you deal with others, those concerned with your own ability to process information, and those that might be called personal-style data. Let us look at one scheme to categorize nontechnical skills:

Work Oriented Nontechnical Skills

A. Intellectual Skills

1. Overall Ability: Basic capacity to learn and understand. Sometimes referred to as "native intelligence" this is a required characteristic for personal and career development.

2. Practical Judgment: The ability to handle day-to-day factual problems quickly and ac-

curately. On the spot problem-solving where you are presented with information and must digest it to formulate an effective decision.

3. Critical Thinking: Longer term planning and problem solving abilities. The ability to decide what information is important to consider for decision-making in far reaching situations of uncertainty.

4. Verbal Facility: Language and verbal skills. Includes vocabulary knowledge and ease in use of oral and written expression.

5. Conceptual Ability: The ability to think at the conceptual, nonverbal level. Often required for design work.

6. Mental Efficiency: The able use of intellectual abilities. Includes the ability to organize a task for solution.

B. Interpersonal Skills

7. Dominance: The degree of personal assertiveness you exercise in your dealings with others.

8. Self-confidence: Poise and assurance in your everyday business dealings with others.

9. Self-acceptance: Extent to which you are aware of your own feelings and accepting of your own abilities and limitations.

10. Projected Image: Concern with maintaining a favorable impression in the eyes of others. Willingness to "go the ex-

tra mile" in order to maintain effective interpersonal relationships.

11. Perceptiveness: The ability to "read" the emotional states and feelings of others. Ability to assess the impact of your own behavior on others.

12. Tact: Knowledge of effective interpersonal behavior in typical work situations.

13. Problem Solving: Knowledge of typically effective means of dealing with "people problems." Practical judgment in solution of interpersonal problems.

14. Tolerance/Flexibility: Degree of flexibility in dealing with others, particularly where their beliefs and behavior differ from your own.

C. Work-Related Skills

15. Responsibility: Maturity and stability of your application to work. Degree of impulsiveness.

16. Achievement: The amount of drive you have to succeed. Preferred methods of seeking success.

17. Energy: Personal energy level and extent to which this energy is effectively focused on productive work activities.

18. Orderliness: The impression of order and attention to detail you convey to others. Task completion skills.

19. Supervision: Knowledge of typically effective supervisory techniques and personal leadership drive.

20. Sales Comprehension: Knowledge of the basic principles of selling.

One way to assess your nontechnical skills is to identify factors other than the technical abilities necessary to realize your accomplishments. This is a useful procedure if you focus on which nontechnical skills you demonstrated rather than which ones might have been required.

For each accomplishment you have listed, identify the nontechnical skills you demonstrated in getting the job done. You do not need to use the twenty nontechnical skills I have identified, although you may find that they provide some structure.

One way to do this exercise is to look carefully at each accomplishment you have written down and ask yourself the question, "What nontechnical skill was necessary to do this?" It is easy to overlook the fact that a knowledge of how to sell was necessary to get your boss to accept a new idea or that people-reading ability was important in delivering a blockbuster speech.

List X. Your Nontechnical Skills

1. _____

    _____

2. _____

    _____

3. _____

    _____

4. _____

    _____

Abilities + Action = Accomplishments

5. _____

_____

6. _____

_____

7. _____

_____

8. _____

_____

9. _____

_____

10. _____

_____

Perhaps because of his position, Glen found it easier to identify his nontechnical skills than he did the technical ones. When he had completed his task, he was surprised by the similarity and breadth of nontechnical skills required for every accomplishment. He remarked that it would be easier to identify those nontechnical skills he had not demonstrated than it would be to list those that he had used for each accomplishment.

For each accomplishment nontechnical skills such as critical thinking, perceptiveness, self-confidence, achievement, energy, and practical judgment were required.

"I'd never thought of these skills as operating separately from my technical knowledge," Glen remarked. He was right. Like most chemical catalysts, when they are present, they are seldom noticed.

Your technical and nontechnical skills are important in determining your career success. Although it is never easy to take a close look at yourself—particularly when there are readily identifiable "soft spots"—it is important that you do so *before* a prospective employer does. This will allow you to put your best foot forward, to accentuate the positive and give you the incentive to improve in those areas that require your attention.

Chapter 7

More Assessment Techniques

"Be sure to keep a mirror always nigh
In some convenient, handy sort of place
And now and then look squarely in thine eye,
And with thyself keep ever face to face."
—*Face to Face* by John Kendrick Bangs

It would be hard to find anyone who demonstrates high competence in all of the nontechnical skills. Happily it would be just as difficult to find any one job that required a high level of competence in all areas.

Another way to assess your own nontechnical skills is to ask yourself a variety of questions that pertain to each nontechnical skill. Look at each statement below and ask yourself if that statement could be applied to you:

SELF ASSESSMENT QUESTIONNAIRE: IDENTIFYING YOUR NONTECHNICAL SKILLS

1. Overall Ability

(a) You are able to learn effectively and remember new information.

(b) You are able to identify ongoing learning on your part, perhaps as a result of adopting new ideas in your work or personal life.

2. Practical Judgment

(a) When a problem comes to your attention, you are able promptly to devise an effective way to deal with it.

(b) You are seldom ruffled by chance events, feeling that whatever comes up you will be able to deal with it.

3. Critical Thinking

(a) When long-range decisions are called for, you are able to identify the important information to consider in making the decision.

(b) You are able to consider simultaneously a great deal of information.

4. Verbal Facility

(a) You have a sound command of vocabulary, that enables you to communicate with a wide variety of people.

(b) You are able to convince others through verbal persuasion.

5. Conceptual Ability

(a) You are able to learn and understand complex abstract material.

(b) You are able to visualize abstract ideas from written or verbal information.

6. Mental Efficiency

(a) You are able to function at a level indicative of your mental abilities.

(b) You are able to pay attention to a number of pressing matters at the same time.

7. Dominance

(a) You put forward your views forcefully in your dealings with others.

(b) When you have a concern about how things are going,

you are able to put forward this concern in a positive manner.

8. Self-confidence

(a) You are able to convey an air of self-assuredness in dealings with others.

(b) You are able to impress others with your ideas and your confidence in them.

9. Self-acceptance

(a) You have a good idea of your own abilities, particularly when compared to others.

(b) In assessing a situation you are able to determine your ability to handle it.

10. Projected Image

(a) You are aware of your own impact on others when you are dealing with them.

(b) You are familiar with how to change your behavior in order to obtain desired results in dealing with others.

11. Perceptiveness

(a) When you are dealing with others, you are able to "read between the lines" accurately.

(b) You are able to assess how people are feeling from talking to them.

12. Tact

(a) You are familiar with generally accepted courses of action in dealings with others.

(b) In work situations requiring interpersonal decision-making, you are able to select appropriate action from a broad range of possibilities.

13. Problem Solving

(a) When confronted with others' interpersonal problems you are able to deal with them effectively.

(b) You exercise good practical judgment in dealing with "people matters."

14. Tolerance/Flexibility

(a) You are able to regulate your own feelings and actions in dealings with those with whom you do not agree or hold similar values.

(b) You are able to respond in a variety of ways to pressing interpersonal situations.

15. Responsibility

(a) You are strongly committed to the work ethic, are dependable in performing your responsibilities.

(b) You are well regulated in your work behavior and your emotions are under control.

16. Achievement

(a) You desire to succeed in whatever you do, producing tangible results from your efforts.

(b) You have a good grasp of your own achievement style, that is, how it might be directed and in what situations it is likely to flourish.

17. Energy

(a) You have a sound level of personal energy and are able to direct it effectively in work situations.

(b) You are uncomfortable in situations in which there is not enough to do.

18. Orderliness

(a) You are able to organize yourself to achieve whatever you are doing.

(b) You are able to convey a sense of orderliness to others so that they might place greater confidence in your results.

19. Supervision

(a) You have a knowledge of effective supervisory techniques.

(b) You have a strong desire to lead others.

20. Sales Comprehension

(a) You have knowledge of effective selling techniques.

(b) You are able to assess others so that you can match persuasive techniques to the person you are attempting to persuade.

OTHER WAYS TO ASSESS YOUR ABILITIES OR STYLE

It is evident that the methods I have proposed so far for assessing your technical and nontechnical skills suffer from a major shortcoming—you. It is difficult to be accurate if you are at the same time both the person being measured and the measurer. It is not that I am accusing you of conscious distortion in estimating your abilities, but it is difficult to maintain perspective with only one source of data.

Be wary of relying totally on self-estimates in determining your ability. Be equally wary of depending totally on someone else's opinion.

There are several ways you can supplement self-assessment in determining your own technical and nontechnical abilities. Although no method yields objective data (if such a thing really exists), each method provides another perspective on you. Your job is to put together these varying perspectives and come up with the total picture.

One of the best ways is to rely on the assistance of a similarly qualified colleague. It is not important that the person be employed with you on a day-to-day basis. It is important that your colleague be willing to go over the accomplishments you have outlined in order to dig out skill areas you may have overlooked. Do not expect total agreement from such a person. In fact, if you get total agreement, you are either very lucky, or more likely, the other person does not feel comfortable in disagreeing with your interpretation.

It is more difficult to use this type of approach with your nontechnical skills, but there is really little choice but to do so. Rather than selecting an individual whose technical skills you respect as a foil for your self-assessment, try to get help from someone who is competent in nontechnical areas. It may be better to select someone who is not familiar with your technical area.

Alternatively find several people who are interested in doing the same thing and work together in reviewing each other's accomplishments. Once again, work with your confidants to examine your accomplishments—and what these accomplishments show about you.

ASSESSMENTS FOR HIRE

It is at the point of assessing nontechnical skills that some individuals seek professional help. The individual most often selected is an industrial psychologist, although other professionals ranging from career counsellors to management consultants are also used. Like any professional service group, the range of services is broad, as are the quality and the price.

Here are several guidelines you should consider before deciding whether or not you will opt for professional help—and what to look for in any professional you may decide to retain.

1. Make sure you know what it is you want to learn about yourself before paying anyone to help you find it out. Most industrial psychologists do not have the background to assess technical skills (except in their own area), but may be helpful in certain aspects of the nontechnical area. Professional help is most useful and cost-effective when you are unsatisfied with your self-assessment or with the results from other methods such as help from an associate.

2. If you decide to seek professional help, stick with an accredited professional. Most states or provinces regulate the practice of psychology by licensing. It is not a foolproof way to get your money's worth but it does help to weed out some obvious crackpots.

3. In selecting a professional, particularly a psychologist, make certain that he/she is oriented toward business or work rather than more clinical areas. You are most inter-

ested in assessing your abilities in the work domain, not in the more usual helping areas of psychology. Be wary of any professional who claims competence in areas ranging from family counseling to industrial psychology to sensitivity groups.

4. Before you select a particular professional, set up a preliminary meeting to find out what service is provided and how much it will cost. Very often this meeting will cost nothing or very little. If a package deal is being offered make certain you understand what it involves and that you, want and need everything you will be charged for.

5. Ask about the method of data collection to be used. Extensive interviewing is common but so is comprehensive psychological testing used in conjunction with interview. My biases tend toward the latter.

6. What will the final result look like? Will you receive verbal or written feedback, ongoing assistance to deal with weaknesses that are identified, or concrete suggestions for change? The most useful information will be behavioral; that is, it will deal with how you would be expected to perform in a variety of work situations in comparison to others. The least useful information will be general personality indicators couched in psychological jargon.

7. Ask for references. Although the names of previous clients are confidential, they can be released with their permission. Expect that the references you are given will be positive—psychologists are no fools. Ask the references specific questions rather than being satisfied with an "it was great" response.

8. Expect to pay on the order of five hundred to a thousand dollars for assistance, depending on the nature of the service provided. You may be able to obtain an hourly rate for three or four less formal discussion sessions.

9. Do not expect miracles. You are buying another perspective—one that should be less tainted by personal circumstances—as well as some advice about what to do with

what you have got. You will still have to weigh this information with what you already have. You will still have to decide what you are going to do about you.

Professional help in identifying your nontechnical abilities can be very helpful or it may be a waste of time. To avoid mistakes, be certain you know what you want and how you are going to get it.

WHAT TO DO ABOUT WHAT YOU HAVE GOT

If you have gone through the self-assessment just outlined in *CareerScan*, used the services of an industrial psychologist, or are already aware by other means of your technical and nontechnical abilities, you have come a long way in your job search process. But there are other things to keep in mind.

The first thing to remember is the inherent inaccuracy in assessing abilities, no matter which method(s) you have used. Because the factors are so ill-defined and the measurement tools so crude, you can never get even the same degree of accuracy that you get from a bathroom scale measurement of weight. If your estimate is not what you think it should be, do not despair. The inaccuracy may be in the measurement.

The second thing to remember is that your abilities are not static; they are subject to change through experience and training. If you are unhappy with your ability in one or more areas, it is within your power to do something about it. Night school, intensive reading, part- or full-time study—there are many avenues you can use to improve your skills.

After a fifteen year absence from her nursing career during which she had raised a family, Gail attended a career development seminar. Subsequent to the self-assessment sessions, Gail decided not to return to nursing, a career she felt no longer met her needs. Instead she decided to attempt a career as a stockbroker, an area she had dabbled in on a personal basis through the years.

Although she understood the basics of securities transactions, Gail identified two areas that would require attention to maximize her likelihood of success. One was more extensive knowledge about securities, an area she planned to address through a part-time course offered through a securities firm. The other was developing her basic selling skills, a deficiency to be dealt with through extensive reading in selling techniques and several one or two day seminars offered through her local community college.

Unlike needs, your skills are open to change. In fact, you may have to improve your skills to give yourself a reasonable chance of meeting your needs through work.

Chapter 8

Job Assessment

"I . . . chose my wife, as she did her wedding-gown, not for a fine glossy surface, but with such qualities as would wear well."—*The Vicar of Wakefield* by Oliver Goldsmith

In job selection it is important to understand yourself, your technical and nontechnical abilities. (That is the "know thyself" that Plato was half-right about.) It is equally important to know the skills that any prospective job might require. (That is the "know thy job" that Plato forgot.) The match between these two is what determines your success on the job and the likelihood that you will meet your needs through work.

Job assessment applies the same techniques that you used in assessing yourself to any prospective job you might be considering. It is a study of which skills are required (and to what degree) to perform the job well.

Knowing what a job requires will help you to strike a balance between that and what you have to offer.

In the same way as your skills were categorized as technical or nontechnical, the demands of any particular job can be similarly categorized. All you need to do is look at individuals who already work *successfully* at the job and determine which abilities help them in their position. You do not have to be the same as they are, but you will be better off to have or develop the skills they use on the job.

There are a variety of ways to assess a job to determine the skills and levels of skills that it requires. Perhaps the easiest is to refer to a glossary like the *Dictionary of Occupational Titles* that lists nearly every job and the skills required for it. This is a United States Government publication; its Canadian counterpart, the *Canadian Classification and Dictionary of Occupations*, is also helpful. Either is available in major public libraries or government document centers.

The research for both of these publications is extensive and they form a good starting point for studying a specific job. Look at your lists of technical and nontechnical skills to see how they measure up to the demands as outlined in these publications. You will probably note that each of these publications is deficient in listing the nontechnical skills and that the skills that are listed may be too general for your needs. But it is a good place to start.

To get beyond the shortcomings of any encyclopedia, you will have to do some digging. You will have to go to the source—someone, preferably several people, who already works at that job.

In Section I, I described how you could interview several people employed in a job as an aid to understanding needs that might be met by that job. The same technique can be applied here, but the emphasis is on skills rather than needs. Frame your questions in terms of what a person must know in order to do well in the position you are studying. Pay particular attention to nontechnical skills since the interpretation of which ones are important may vary considerably depending on who you are talking to.

Try to get the individuals you are interviewing to identify what things make the difference between an individual who does well or does poorly in the job you are considering. What skills are critical, important, desirable, and so on.

It is sometimes difficult to get the person you want to meet to agree to meet with you—especially if they are busy. Assure them that you are not looking for a job and that you do not want any help in finding one. Be persistent. As an alternative, consider attending part-time or evening extension courses offered through your local university, community college, or technical institute. These courses are a good place to meet fellow students from a variety of occupations and often the instructors are the very people you wanted to meet.

Dean was a thirty-seven-year-old controller for a multinational oil company. For the last few years, he had become increasingly dissatisfied with his current job. After extensive self-analysis, he concluded that his present job did not sufficiently meet his needs, particularly in the areas of economics and competition.

While still maintaining his job with the oil company, he began to pursue contacts in a work area he felt held promise for a future job, financial consulting with junior oil and gas companies. He met informally with representatives of many junior companies and, as he did so, began to see an area that he could develop—venture capital acquisition.

Although venture capital was not an area in which Dean was particularly proficient, he was able to identify the few technical skills that would require brushing up.

Six months later when Dean made his move, he was thoroughly knowledgeable about his new industry—and had a number of contacts to ensure his success.

For certain professional positions it is as important to consider how the skills were acquired as it is to understand the skills themselves. Some professions (accounting, law, etc.) require that skills be learned through formal schooling, demonstrating competence is not enough. This may be a limiting factor in your choice of such a job.

When considering a job opportunity, look first to see if it meets the needs you want to have met through work. Then look again to see if the skills demanded by the job match what you have to offer.

SECTION II: SUMMARY

1. Formulating your career on the basis of a life goal is unrealistic. Careers are best formed by ensuring that each job meets needs that you have decided are important.

2. You are selected for a job because of your demonstrated abilities in technical and nontechnical areas.

3. There are a variety of ways to assess your abilities and it is important that you do so before opting for a specific job.

4. Your accomplishments are important for what others will infer about you from them.

5. There are a variety of opportunities for you to meet your needs through work.

6. It is important for you to analyze potential jobs in terms of what technical or nontechnical skills they will demand of you and what needs they will meet.

Section III

Getting a Job

"There are two things to aim at in life: first to get what you want; and, after that, to enjoy it. Only the wisest of mankind achieve the second."
—*Afterthoughts* by Logan Smith

— you are seeking a job after being absent from the work force for a number of years.

— you have decided that your current job does not meet your needs and plan to seek a better alternative.

— you are uncertain how to go about seeking a job in a professional manner.

— you have blanketed the world with resumes with no positive results.

— you have difficulty getting beyond the personal interview stage of the recruiting process.

— you are uncertain about what recruiters are really looking for.

— you already have set ideas about how to get a job and are not prepared to change your mind.

— you are uncertain about what you have to offer a prospective employer. (You may want to go back to Section II.)

— you are satisfied with your present job and have little intention of changing your job within the next two years.

Chapter 9

A New Beginning

"The most reliable way to anticipate the future is by understanding the present."—*Megatrends* by John Naisbitt

John had noticed Sally at the party and wanted to get to know her. Throughout the party, he mustered his courage, finally getting her in a position where he could initiate a private conversation.

"Hi," he said. "My name's John Archer. I'd like to get to know you, maybe do something together sometimes.

"I'm twenty-seven years old," he continued, "and I've had a bit of experience with women—but of course they weren't quite like you. I went with a woman from my home town—her name was Belinda—for three years. We didn't ever make love during that whole time. I don't know, she said she wasn't ready yet.

"I know that I'm no great looker but then again that's not what some women look for in a man. I had a girlfriend about six months ago—her name was Grace—who said I was one of the best looking men she knew. We made love all the time—at least for a while.

"I've got a college education, majored in geology, make twenty-eight thousand dollars a year, and own my car outright. I failed grade seven but made the honor role in my sophomore college year. I still live at home with my aged mother but I'm hoping to be able to leave in the next year or so.

"What do you say? Would you like to go to dinner on Saturday night?"

What are the chances that John will get that date? At best he will probably get a polite refusal. More likely Sally will require assistance to leave the party because she will be overcome with laughter.

What has John Archer revealed about himself? Is the information all that damning? Is it different from information that many of us *could* reveal about ourselves? Probably not. What is different is the manner that John has chosen to reveal information about himself and the fact that he has told everything all at once.

In job seeking most people use John's method—often with the same results you might expect John to get with Sally. Like John most job seekers succeed in spite of what they do, with credit for their success going more to the ineptitude of the recruiter than the job-seeking skill of the applicant.

Most people fail in their search for a job because they fail to manage information about themselves that they share with prospective employers.

A firm specializing in executive recruiting conducted research to study how well candidates who had earlier been placed in certain jobs would fare if they were anonymously entered into the job selection process again for similar jobs. Since these candidates had already been through the complete selection process in their successful search for a job, a great deal of information—good and bad—was already known about them. All that information—except the fact that they had gotten the job—was available to the recruiter doing the initial culling for the new position.

Surprisingly many of the executives who had previously been successful in their real search for a job were less successful in this mock-up study. In trying to find out why, it became clear that they were successful in the first case because they had been very prudent in revealing information about themselves to the recruiter. They had not revealed negative or neutral information about themselves early in the recruiting process. When, as in the study, that information was available to the recruiter from the beginning of the assignment, the executives were much less successful in surviving the initial culling of unsatisfactory candidates.

During the initial phases of the job-search process, you cannot make the recruiter say yes. Your job is to prevent the recruiter from saying no.

The job-search process is a difficult, sometimes unpleasant, even embarrassing process. I know some people describe it as challenging and exhilarating, a chance to really "show your stuff." They are usually the same people who have never had seriously to look for a job. Searching for a job is not easy—but it is not impossible either—and you can succeed in finding the job you need.

It is easier to look for a job—and you will be more successful at it—if you avoid the mistakes that everybody else makes. You do not have to be better than the other candidates to get the job you want. You *do* have to appear to be better. You can do that by managing the information that you reveal about yourself.

Let us look at how most people search for a job. First, they prepare a resume that usually includes when and where they worked, their previous job responsibilities, educational background, basic personal information, and names of references. Second, they forward this resume in response to advertisements, leads provided by others, or blindly to employers they feel may be interested in them. With their resume they usually include a covering letter repeating all the important points in their resume. If the advertisement requests someone who is energetic, loyal, and a good communicator, they make sure that they say in their covering letter that they have these character-istics. The truly creative ones will vary the order of these characteristics in their letter from the list provided in the advertisement, perhaps describing themselves as a good com-municator, loyal, and energetic!

Having done these two things, the typical job searcher sits back and waits for the phone to ring or anxiously checks each day's mail for a job offer—or at least an invitation to interview. In due time they usually receive a "Dear John Archer" form letter—a polite refusal.

Typical job searchers look for a job in a way that practically guarantees they will be overlooked. They look for a job by going through the same motions as everyone else.

Let us look at the other side of the coin—what employers do when they are searching for an employee. The employer usually starts out with a vague idea of what the prospective employee should look like, sometimes knowing little more than someone is wanted who can "do the job." An advertise-ment is drafted, perhaps by the personnel department, describ-ing the characteristics of the desired person.

In response to an advertisement, or perhaps through less formal means, the employer receives a number of resumes, perhaps a large number. All the resumes include a covering letter telling the reader that, perhaps just by happy coincidence, all candi-dates exactly fit the description in the advertisement—they are good communicators, loyal, and energetic.

Somebody who works for the employer—if it is a large company, someone in the personnel department—receives all of these resumes and letters, and is assigned the task of rejecting the majority of candidates so that the ultimate decision-maker will have an easier job selecting the successful candidate. The initial reader is usually given a general descrip-tion of the position, what to look for, and what to avoid in prospective candidates.

Initially, since the letters all read the same (except for the spelling mistakes in copying the list of important characteristics from the advertisement), they are ignored. Each resume is screened for twenty to thirty seconds to see if it can be rejected for some reason. That reason may be length of experience, sex or age or marital status (illegal but still used), direct experience in a selected area, etc. Most "John Archer" applicants do not make it beyond this initial screening. The few who do are those who have not provided the negative information that would have screened them out. They are not the winners but those who have not provided information that could have identified them as losers.

Most people provide too much potentially negative information about themselves too early in the selection process. As a consequence they never get the opportunity to show their true colors.

Think for a minute about long-term friends (lovers, spouses) that you have known. What do you know about them? Chances are that there are some things you like about them but there are also some things that drive you crazy. Your spouse may snore; your friend may be a cheapskate; your lover may be half-hearted about Bach—as well as having many positive or redeeming characteristics. Now ask yourself what things you discovered first about these people? Chances are, it was the more positive things. You realized and tolerated the negative things *after* you had an opportunity to balance them against more positive characteristics. If you knew the negative things first, or even at the same time as the more positive characteristics, you might have decided not to pursue the relationship and therefore not have discovered the things you really like about the other person. It is the same way with recruiting—only more so.

In the initial stages of the recruiting process, the job of a recruiter is to screen out applicants. This is accomplished by putting a disproportionate amount of weight on negative information available about a candidate. During the later stages this weighting reverses itself—but by then most candidates are not around to benefit from the switch. To make it worse, most recruiters are unaware of how they weigh information—they just do it that way.

The typical job applicant thinks that by giving a recruiter as much personal information as possible, the odds of being hired improve. The professional recruiter, they reason, will properly weight this information, matching strengths and weaknesses to get a balanced perspective. In fact, the reverse is true. Providing all of your information all at once, "The John Archer Syndrome," practically guarantees that you will be screened out of many job competitions. To be successful, you have to pay more attention to what you are telling about yourself, as well as how and when you tell what.

The unwritten rules that govern male-female amorous relationships will stand you in better stead during the recruiting process than most of the written rules about how to get a job.

Most people make their first mistake in searching for a job by assuming that the basic unit of getting a job is an effective letter or a blockbuster resume. As a result, they usually compose the kind of resume that is ignored. (That is equally true of those who hire others to write their resume for them.) Such resumes are usually nothing more than a correctly spelled employment record coupled with educational and personal data.

As we will see later, the right kind of letter or resume is important in searching for a job, but preparing your letter or a resume ought to be the last thing you do when you start your search for a job. Your basic tool in searching for a job is your skills. People make two mistakes in describing this basic unit.

1. An almost universal mistake made by job searchers, including some very senior job searchers, is confusing where they have worked and what they have done with their actual skills. Your skills are what you have. Where you have worked and what you have done has given you the opportunity to learn, practice, and demonstrate these skills. A prospective employer is interested in your skills not some ragtag employment history.

2. Most people think that it is sufficient to state that they possess a certain skill and that others will believe this.

When I ask candidates to describe one of their best characteristics, they invariably answer "good with people." I often wonder if everybody is good with people, why is the world falling apart? As I stated in Section II, your skills are defined by others through inference, and most job seekers provide a recruiter precious little on which to base a positive inference.

STEPS TO JOB SEARCH SUCCESS

There are three general steps in a successful job search. They are not difficult but they are time-consuming. Here are the steps.

1. Identifying what skills and other personal characteristics you have to offer.

2. Proving these skills by identifying accomplishments or specific examples that will cause others to infer that you have these skills.

3. Marketing these skills in your written and oral job search— letters, resumes, and telephone or personal interviews.

Usually the first two steps are done simultaneously because identifying an accomplishment usually leads you to a skill, or identifying a skill leads you to specify accomplishments requiring such a skill.

Searching for a job is an exercise in selling yourself. You begin a successful selling campaign by identifying what you have to sell and then deciding how you are going to sell it.

1. Deciding What You Have To Sell

Forget for the time being about resumes, letters, and all the other necessary paraphernalia associated with searching for a job. Let us focus on you.

The critical thing about you is your skills, because you could have practiced these skills at companies other than the ones at which you were employed. The companies that employed you and your job responsibilities are incidental to specifying your skills.

Imagine that you have never worked for any company; you have been self-employed. The companies that purchased your services gave you the opportunity to demonstrate certain skills. The skills are *yours*. They do not belong to any employer—past or future. Even if an employer assisted you to learn something, the important thing is what you have learned—your skills.

> John Markle was a thirty-six-year-old news manager with a national news organization. Starting with the company after graduating from college at age twenty-two, John held a variety of positions ranging from copywriter to regional manager of news services. He had performed duties such as interviewing public figures, writing and editing news copy, staff selection and supervision, training of junior personnel, budgeting, and formulating corporate policy.
>
> Arlice Farkle was a thirty-six-year-old senior editor at a major international book publishing company. She had joined the company three years before. Prior to that, she held positions as a copywriter for a radio station, publishers' representative, and franchise holder/manager for a retail bookselling chain. Over the course of her career, she had performed duties such as interviewing public figures, writing and editing news copy, staff selection and supervision, training of junior personnel, budgeting, and formulating corporate policy.

The first step in getting the job you want is to be very clear about what you have to offer.

There are many ways to determine your skills and other job-related personal characteristics. If you have difficulty in determining yours, refer to Section II of *CareerScan*.

2. Proving Your Worth

Deciding what you are worth is important. Proving your worth is even more important. Your value to a prospective employer depends on your ability to convince an employer that you are valuable. In marketing terms you are worth what you are able to convince someone that you are worth.

You will be most successful at getting a job if you are able to convince a recruiter that you can do the things required in the new job. That means demonstrating that you have already successfully done those things or, at least, something directly related to those things.

Most job seekers are poor at proving their worth. They either list everything they have done and expect that others will figure out what they are worth or they tell others what they are worth and expect that they will be believed. Either method is unconvincing.

Before you think about how you can prove your worth to others, consider how others prove their worth to you. On what basis do you decide that a person has a certain skill or personal characteristic? If you are like most, you do it by inferences formed on the basis of what you see or hear—the behavior exhibited by the other person. This is the way we form inferences or impressions of others in all of our work and nonwork life. It is your job to use this general principle to your advantage in managing the impressions that others will form about you as you progress through a recruiting assignment.

For example, if everyone knows that you are searching for an honest person, most interested people will describe themselves as honest. You will probably become somewhat jaded to these assertions after you hear them often enough. But, when you drop your wallet in a crowd and a stranger returns it to you unopened, that stranger does not have to assert honesty. You infer that the stranger is honest and that inference is immeasurably stronger than any convincing the stranger might try to do. It is the same in searching for a job.

In searching for a job most people fail to provide the evidence that will influence others to form favorable inferences about them.

Eric was a twenty-six-year-old computer programmer and junior systems analyst. He was extremely capable at his job, was thought of as a creative and thoroughly effective professional.

In his search for a new position Eric answered an advertisement in a local paper. As part of his covering letter Eric described himself as "a thoroughly experienced senior programmer, well versed in Fortran and Cobol programming, familiar with detailed software design and modification, able to relate well with technical and non-technical staff."

Ernie was a twenty-seven-year-old computer programmer and junior systems analyst. He was totally inept and most projects he had been associated with were failures.

In his search for a new position Ernie answered an advertisement in a local paper. As part of his covering letter Ernie described himself as, "a thoroughly experienced senior programmer, well versed in Fortran and Cobol programming, familiar with detailed software design and modification, able to relate well with technical and nontechnical staff."

In most recruitment situations the good candidate does not provide evidence that is a great deal different from the poor candidate. As long as both candidates speak in vague generalities, listing their personal characteristics or job descriptions, the good candidate is placed at considerable disadvantage. It is true that this disadvantage will probably disappear after a skilled recruiter conducts personal interviews or does a detailed examination of both backgrounds—but most good candidates never get to that part of the recruiting process. They are disqualified, along with many poor candidates, early in the process.

There is a problem in proving your worth. Most of life is not like losing your wallet in a crowd, with that excellent opportunity to make inferences about the finder (or keeper!). In searching for a job the recruiter has not seen you working and must make inferences about your personal characteristics and abilities on the basis of indirect evidence—oft times very sketchy evidence. You can help the recruiter—and yourself— by making certain that the right kind of evidence is available. Evidence that counts will ensure that the inferences made about you by the recruiter are as positive as you would like them to be.

You manage the impressions or inferences others form about you by managing the information you make available to others about yourself.

To influence the inferences that recruiters form about you, you will want to provide information that is as close as possible to you at your best. To make the best impact, you should provide information that shows what you did and how well you did it. Look at the examples below.

Example 1

A. I have sound geological skills and am very knowledgeable about state-of-the-art mining exploration techniques.

B. As Chief Geologist for a multinational mining company, I developed a new drilling method using laser and high pressure water technology. This reduced drilling costs by seventeen percent and drilling time by twenty-five percent.

Example 2

A. I have excellent interpersonal and selling skills.

B. As manager of a seven person sales office of a national firm, I mediated disputes between sales persons sharing a common sales territory and handled customer complaints.

I maintained a nil staff turnover rate over a two year period and increased market penetration by eight percent.

Example 3

A. I am well organized and plan my time effectively.

B. I managed a hectic three person business specializing in direct mail advertising for more than thirty clients. During this same period I attended evening classes in order to complete my MBA degree and mothered a happy family of three young children.

What inferences could you make on the basis of the three examples? You have probably read or heard countless examples similar to Statement A. They represent a value judgment by the speaker with the vain hope that the listener will share in the belief that is asserted.

Statement B is different. Each one makes no direct claim about the speaker. It states what has happened and leaves it to the listener to make the inference about what kind of individual has made it happen. B statements are both specific and verifiable. Response B from each example represents the kind of information you should reveal to a recruiter about yourself through letter, resume, and interview. The control you are able to exert comes from the choice of activity you choose to highlight and the manner in which you detail the activity.

In job searching you cannot tell someone what you are like and expect that they will believe you. You can only provide information about what you have done and leave the listener (or reader) to draw their own conclusions. An example is worth a thousand words.

Chapter 10

Proving Your Worth

"The fly has other wondrous accomplishments, too, not
the least of which is being able to land on the ceiling.
—*To Know a Fly* by Vincent Dethier

The basic building block of job seeking is you—your skills and
personal characteristics. In getting ready to prepare your
resume and letters that you will use in your job search, you
must:

1. Identify your skills and personal characteristics.
2. Be able to prove these skills and personal characteristics
   to others.

IDENTIFYING YOUR ACCOMPLISHMENTS

If you have completed Section II of *CareerScan*, you have
already had some practice in identifying your skills by a
process that made you focus on your accomplishments. Accomplishments in the job search process are nothing more than
concrete examples of your skills that will create a favorable
impression when someone hears about them. Your accomplishments are the basic building blocks you will use in your job
search process. Everything else—your letters, resumes, and
interviews—is based on the proper identification and expression of your accomplishments.

The accomplishments you identified in Section II were written so that they were meaningful for you. To be meaningful for others, to have others make the proper inference about you, you have to phrase your accomplishments differently, in a way that conveys exactly what you want the other person to infer about you.

Here are some guidelines for writing your accomplishments:

1. Action Talks So Talk Action
   Your accomplishments should include an action verb expressed in the past tense. Examples of such action verbs are planned, implemented, sold, supervised, organized, drafted, etc. Look for an "ed" at the end of the verb.

2. Burn Your Old Job Description
   Your accomplishments should list one or perhaps two related things you have done. Listing a variety of general activities does not create the impact you want. Do not say, "I worked in areas such as financial control, budgeting, and receivables." Tell the reader specifically what you did.

3. Remember Your RBI Average
   Your accomplishments should include some statement of how well you did the particular thing you are highlighting. This might include an indication of a saving in money or time, feedback received from others, or some other statement that leaves the reader with the impression that the job was well done.

4. Who You Did What With
   The accomplishment should be tied to your work circumstances at the time of the accomplishment. This may include the name of the company or a generic reference to the type of employer as well as your position title or generic title. For example, you might say, "As Chief Snake Trainer for the Bombay Circus . . ." or alternately, "As a manager of animal training for a major international circus. . . ."

5. Just as she fell down the elevator shaft . . .
   Write your accomplishment in a manner that encourages the reader to read it. Starting sentences with *as, since,* or

while is a good way to do this because it pulls the reader along to your main idea.

There are really three main parts to an accomplishment. The first part or Introduction provides information to the reader about your work or nonwork circumstances at the time of the accomplishment and also pulls the reader into the accomplishment by means of its engaging writing style. The second part includes the Action Verb and description of what you actually completed. The third part concerns the Effectiveness of your actions. Here are three examples.

Introduction   While teaching primary students at an inner city elementary school,

Action Verb   developed an intramural physical education program for "disadvantaged" senior students.

Effectiveness   Program led to reduced truancy and drop-out rate and is still in place six years later.

Introduction   In order to foster self-development,

Action Verb   completed a grueling physical challenge program for executives. Program included mountain climbing, backpacking, and wilderness survival.

Effectiveness   After course completion, was asked to participate in instructor program in subsequent years.

Introduction   As Manager of Financial Services for a fully integrated oil company,

Action Verb   designed a computerized financial reporting system used by three subsidiary companies with assets totalling $750M.

Effectiveness   System reduced reporting time by 10%.

TESTING YOUR KNOWLEDGE

Here are several examples of accomplishments. Read each one carefully to see if it contains the three major parts outlined above.

1. I worked for the Racearound Taxi Company. My job was to deliver passengers and packages in the downtown and light industrial areas of a major metropolitan area. I was promoted to area supervisor after three years.

2. As Senior Architect in charge of business development for Haight, Thornebury, and Sandpiper, obtained three major development projects totalling $750M within one year in fierce competition with international firms.

3. Started up and managed three new drycleaning businesses in less than two years.

4. I had responsibility for managing a pharmaceutical sales branch office of three salespersons with annual sales of $3M.

5. I have experience with cost analysis, budgeting, financial management, and critical path planning.

DOING IT FOR YOURSELF

It is time for you to begin writing your own accomplishments. It's helpful if you have already done some of the initial work in Section II, but if you have not, go ahead anyway. Remember that you are identifying your accomplishments in order to have the reader form favorable inferences about your abilities. The question to ask yourself about each accomplishment is, "What does this say to the reader about me?" Keep in mind the important points of writing accomplishments that have already been outlined.

A final hint is to keep your sentences and paragraphs short and easy to read. This might necessitate using abbreviations (CEO instead of chief executive officer) or figures and symbols (10% instead of ten percent). Guard against trying to include too much in each accomplishment. The best approach is to describe a singular specific event.

It is crucial that you take the time necessary to write and edit your accomplishments. Accomplishments are the basic building blocks of an effective search for a job; they are used in letters, resumes, and interviews. They are important enough that if you have to rent a hotel room to get away from distractions in order to write them you should do it.

Most people report that writing and editing the accomplishments takes from five to ten hours to properly complete—but it cannot be done in a single sitting. It is best to set aside some specific times—a weekend, several evenings, or your lunch periods for a week. Remember that you can focus on your work or nonwork activities.

Accomplishments

1. _____

_____

_____

_____

2. _____

_____

_____

_____

3. _____

_____

_____

_____

4. _____

_____

_____

_____

5. _____

_____

_____

_____

6. _____

_____

_____

_____

7. _____

_____

_____

_____

8. _____

_____

_____

_____

9. _____

_____

_____

_____

10. _____

_____

_____

_____

11. _____

_____

_____

_____

Glen, the forty-year-old controller of a Fortune 500 company who described his accomplishments in Section II, revised them in accordance with the five points of accomplishment writing.

1. As Manager of Financial Services for a fully integrated oil company, designed a computerized financial reporting system used by three subsidiary companies with assets totalling $750M. System reduced reporting time 10%.

2. Working with external consultants, developed a plan for the use of microcomputers within a multibranch banking system. System was adopted with a projected annual saving of 23%.

3. While employed as Manager of Financial Services, worked with other corporate branches to develop an improved inventory system for petrochemical by-products. System reduced shipping delays and assisted in increased market penetration.

4. On a request basis by Brainfull University, instructed a graduate class in advanced financial management. After the first offering, class was oversubscribed every subsequent year.

5. As Assistant Manager of Corporate Affairs for a multinational oil company, worked closely with Human Resources Division to develop an Executives in Training program for recent college graduates. To date this program has produced two VPs and a great many successful managers.

6. In order to foster self-development, completed a grueling physical challenge program for executives. Program included mountain climbing, backpacking, and wilderness survival. After course completion was asked to participate in instructor program in subsequent years.

7. Worked with Personnel Division to develop innovative peer-based performance appraisal system for financial division of a multibranch bank. System has since been adopted by all other corporate divisions.

8. As Manager of Financial Services for a multibranch bank, developed and implemented complicated take-

over procedures of a competitor's operation. System has stood the test of three unsuccessful lawsuits.

9. For *Financial Outlook Quarterly* and *Daguerre's Digest,* wrote two complex financial articles dealing with the future of financial reporting systems. One article has been selected for reprinting in an upccming textbook for graduate students.

Glen was also able to identify several other accomplishments and included them with the revisions of his earlier work.

10. As Volunteer Fundraising Director for Brainfull University, initiated an innovative legacy program that has resulted in a 12% increase in corporate donations over the past two years.

11. After developing a plan to increase volunteers for foster parent organization, implemented the program over a two-year period increasing numbers of volunteers by 10%/year.

12. Completed MBA from Brainfull University, graduating at the top of a class of 75. Thesis on financial modeling systems was selected for major student award at graduation.

13. As antique automotive mechanic and collector, restored a 1928 Packard, receiving first prize at local level and honorable mention at regional competition.

Jane, the teacher referred to in Section II who was returning to her career after an absence of several years, produced the following list after modifying her accomplishments.

1. As teacher with the Mulberry Board of Education, I set up and implemented an innovative enrichment pro-

gram for gifted children. This program was well received by students and parents and has since formed the basis for similar programs throughout the system.

2. Completed an innovative teaching program at Head-full University graduating in the top 15% of my class. Program focused on individualizing instruction and design of alternative teaching methods.

3. While teaching primary students at an inner city elementary school, developed an intramural physical education program for "disadvantaged" senior students. Program led to reduced truancy and dropout rate and is still in place six years later.

4. Was asked by regional teacher's association to develop and instruct a time management program for novice teachers. Program was well attended and over-subscribed on successive offerings.

5. While taking a leave from active teaching to raise two active toddlers, completed three classes toward a Master's degree in Education, placing near the top of all classes.

6. Pioneered use of revised reading program for an urban school system of 25,000 students. The report that I prepared on the program formed the basis for system's decision not to adopt the revised program.

7. Published an article entitled: "Designing Effective Language Arts Programs for Young Children" in a regional magazine for teachers.

TESTING YOUR ACCOMPLISHMENTS

The acid test for your accomplishments is what others will infer about you as a result of reading or listening to them. You should test this out in some manner so that you are certain that your descriptions of your accomplishments communicate to others what you want them to communicate. Another important point is to make sure you have covered all your bases by highlighting accomplishments that reflect all the abilities required for the position you are seeking.

One way to test your written accomplishments is to try to understand them in the eyes of the beholder. Itemize what inferences you think the reader might make about you. An even better way is to share your accomplishments with several other individuals whose opinions you respect and ask them what inferences your accomplishments foster for them. With such feedback you can revise and polish descriptions to ensure that they are not ambiguous and that they cover the areas necessary to obtain the jobs that you will be pursuing.

Another way to test your accomplishments is to check that you have covered the areas that are important in nearly all jobs. Sometimes in focusing on specific abilities for a particular job, people forget this. Some of these areas are:

1. *Interpersonal Skills.* Have you provided evidence that you get along well with people, are able to deal effectively with a variety of people, and can handle people in difficult situations?

2. *Intellectual Ability.* Have you demonstrated that you are a quick learner, able to catch on to new ideas easily, and adept at applying principles that you have learned?

3. *Organizational Ability.* What accomplishments have you detailed that will communicate to the reader that you organize yourself well, are able to handle a number of tasks simultaneously? Have you shown yourself as a good task completer?

4. *Supervisory Skills.* Have you given the reader reason to infer that you can motivate others, delegate responsibility effectively, be firm but fair? Can you demonstrate that you bring out the best in others?

5. *Practical Judgment.* Can you demonstrate that you have a sound ability to deal with problems as they arise and that you can function in an environment that requires alertness and flexibility?

6. *Communications Skills.* What accomplishment have you detailed that will give the reader confidence that you communicate well with others? Have you given evidence of skill in written as well as oral communication?

7. *Results Orientation.* Have you phrased your accomplishments in such a manner that the reader infers that you are concerned with results or are enthused with a bottom line accountability?

MARKETING YOUR ACCOMPLISHMENTS

Once you have gone through the effort of detailing your accomplishments—of proving that you are what you want others to believe you are—you still have to decide how to use this information in your job search. You have identified what you have to offer, have evidence that you have the required skills, and are now at the stage of marketing this information in the most efficient manner.

The least efficient way to look for a job is by using exactly the same method as everybody else. That is the method that ensures your job search campaign will face maximum competition. To be successful you must subvert the usual job search process in a way that ensures you do not alienate those who make recruiting decisions.

At an early stage of my search for a university faculty position, I decided to develop a very unusual resume as an attention getter. Using a commercial artist, I created a comic book. The left side of the page included cartoon drawings of myself doing a variety of things. The right side of the page included standard resume information. My comic book resume was printed on electrifying multicolored paper.

This approach was not successful. At least it was not nearly as successful as my naive enthusiasm dictated that it should be. It was only several years later that I overheard a chance remark between two colleagues from an institution receiving my comic book. It seems that the feelings about the resume were—creative . . . yes, novel . . . yes, eyecatching . . . yes. But would you really want *that* kind of individual working for you?

The information you present in your job search campaign must be somewhat different from that used by others but still thoroughly professional. The information must be presented in such a way that it is not considered as bragging. You do this by concentrating on your accomplishments.

To be successful in your job search campaign you will have to walk the line between being so usual that you bore or so unusual that you alarm.

If you have spent the time and effort required to compose, edit, and test your accomplishments, you have already done the hard work as far as the written part of searching for a job is concerned. Now you must decide how to package these accomplishments so that they will exert a sustained impact.

In searching for a position you want to provide just enough positive information to keep the employer interested in you but not so much that the employer will feel comfortable in screening you out. You want to tease the employer, to leave the impression that there are always better things about you just around the corner. To do that effectively, you will have to rethink the use of your resume.

Although a resume *is* a major part of job searching, the typical resume is wrong and is used at the wrong time. To be effective in your job search, you will have to avoid both of these mistakes.

I will deal with the right kind of resume later in this section. For now let us put the use of a resume—even a good kind of resume (that is, the kind I will show you how to write!)—into perspective.

Most people send a resume, sometimes even a very good resume, in reply to a job advertisement or when they suspect that an employer may have an unadvertised job vacancy. Even if your resume is a blockbuster, this is the wrong time to wave it around. You want to tantalize, to tease, and you cannot do that by doing a "John Archer."

Depending on their size, most companies receive a number of solicited and unsolicited resumes each week. As a consequence they usually have well established procedures to deal with them. Usually these procedures involve forwarding the resumes to a relatively junior officer of the company, often a secretary in the personnel department, with a standard "thanks, but don't call us" form letter returned for effort.

That is not to say that employers do not want your resume. Of course they do. Resumes provide employers with a low risk data bank from which they can pick and choose (or not choose) as they wish. But it is simply not the right tactic to send your resume as the first step in your job search. You have not done all this groundwork to be filed away in a data bank.

You need another strategy to make your first written contact with a potential employer. Rather than a resume, that contact should be a letter—but a very special kind of letter.

Chapter 11

The Action Letter

"The best way is to make your letters safe. I never wrote a letter in all my life that would commit me, and demmy sir, I have had some experience of women."
—*Pendennis* by William Makepeace Thackeray

A letter is better than a resume for several reasons. First, there are less well established mechanisms within most companies to deal with personally addressed letters. This increases the chance that someone in a position to influence your employment will actually look at the letter. Second, a letter is not expected to contain everything about you and therefore allows you to focus on your strengths in terms of the position that interests you. Third, and perhaps most important, everybody else sends resumes.

A well-written job search letter allows you to put your best foot forward without exposing your whole body!

The best way to understand a well written action letter is to look at an example. I will base this example on Glen, our Fortune 500 controller. In this case Glen is responding to an advertisement placed by a recruiting company for a financial services manager with an international automotive rental conglomerate. The advertisement stresses strong computer skills, aggressiveness, and staff management ability.

You will note that Glen uses personalized stationery. This is not a prerequisite for success, but it does enhance your application—particularly for senior positions.

Glen R. Dollars
12445 Hopeful Road
Finance, North America
Ph. (555) 555-5555

September 29, 19XX

Mr. Head Hunter
Global Executive Recruiting Ltd.
12345 Pathos Blvd.
Opportunity City, North America

Dear Mr. Hunter,

As Manager of Financial Services for a fully integrated oil company, I designed a computerized financial reporting system used by three subsidiary
companies with assets totalling $750M. This system
reduced reporting time by 10 percent.

Since you advertised for a Financial Services Manager well versed in computer applications, you may be
interested in other aspects of my career:

— Developed an innovative peer based performance
  appraisal system for the financial division of a
  multibranch bank. System has since been adopted
  by all other corporate divisions.

— For Financial Outlook Quarterly and Daguerre's
  Digest wrote two complex financial articles
  dealing with the future of financial reporting
  systems. One article has been selected for reprinting in an upcoming textbook for graduate
  students.

— As Manager of Financial Services for a multibranch bank, developed and implemented complicated takeover procedures of a competitor's operation. System has withstood three unsuccessful lawsuits.

- Working with external consultants, developed a plan for the use of microcomputers within a multibranch banking system. System was adopted with a projected annual saving of 23%.

- On a request basis by a major Midwestern university, instructed a graduate class in advanced financial management. After the first offering the class was oversubscribed every subsequent year.

- Completed MBA degree from Brainfull University, graduating at the top of a class of 75. Thesis on financial modeling systems was selected for major student award at graduation.

I would like to meet with you to discuss this position in greater depth. I will plan to call you within the next ten days to see if it is possible to arrange a mutually convenient time.

Sincerely,

Glen R. Dollars

What does not appear in Glen's letter is as important as what does appear. Glen does not waste time heralding his attributes. He demonstrates them by referring to what he has accomplished. He does not provide a great deal of information about his previous employers. He sells himself—not his last job.

You will note that all of Glen's accomplishments do not appear in his letter. Nor should they. The secret in writing a good introductory letter such as Glen's is to select those accomplishments that are likely to have the biggest impact on the reader. What you select does not have to be what you see as your strongest assets. Rather, what you provide as accomplishments should reflect those abilities that you think will be most important for the job you are trying to get.

There is no need to present your accomplishments in chronological order. In fact, your letter does not have to contain any activities that are part of your current job. That is the beauty of the letter approach over the resume. The letter deals with you and your abilities in terms of the demands of the job you want—not a blow by blow description of where you have worked and what you were supposed to have done.

The letter puts the control of information in your court. It does not tell everything about you or give all of the information an employer will need to decide if you are the right person for the job. The letter says you *may* be right for the job and, more importantly, it does not say you are wrong. At this introductory point in the job search process, that is the best you can hope for.

Let us analyze the parts of the introductory letter a bit more carefully so that you will be better at creating your own.

1. *The Grabber.* The first thing you want to do in your introductory letter is to get the attention of the reader, to provide some motivation for the reader to continue reading. You do that by presenting your most important accomplishment first—important in terms of what the employer is looking for. You may use one major accomplishment or two shorter ones. Look at Glen's example below.

> As Manager of Financial Services for a fully integrated oil company, I designed a computerized financial reporting system used by three subsidiary companies with assets totalling $750. This system reduced reporting time by 10%.

In this case Glen has decided to focus on his experience with computerized financial reporting. In a simple manner he demonstrates the extent of his involvement—and his success.

2. *Transition.* After you have the attention of your reader, focus and maintain that attention with a short transition paragraph. Look again at Glen's example.

> Since you advertised for a Financial Services Manager well versed in computer applications, you may be interested in other aspects of my career:

This transition paragraph focuses the reader's attention on the accomplishment you have described in the previous paragraph of your letter and explains the purpose of your letter—you are interested in a job.

It is not necessary that this paragraph refer to a specific job, unless you are seeking a position that has been specifically advertised. In the case of Glen's seeking a job that has not been advertised, he might have said,

> Because you might be interested in someone with this level of financial and computer expertise, you may be interested in other aspects of my career.

3. *Accomplishments.* In the third section of your letter detail from three to five of your accomplishments that are

most relevant to the position that interests you. You can use the accomplishment exactly as you wrote it earlier, or modify it slightly for the position you are seeking. Resist the urge to put in too many accomplishments; that is the most common mistake with letters of this sort. Remember that the purpose of your letter is not to tell everything about you—just enough to keep the other person interested.

4. *What Next?* Do not simply end your letter with a thank you. Be clear in specifying what is going to happen next. Are you going to sit by patiently and wait for the employer to call you or are you going to do something to ensure that there will be a next step? Either method is acceptable in certain circumstances. Here is the section from Glen's letter.

I would like to meet with you to discuss this position in greater depth. I plan to call you within the next ten days to see if it is possible to arrange a mutually convenient time.

This is an assertive but not pushy conclusion. It is clear that the next step is up to Glen; he will call to make an appointment. He is not demanding an appointment, although he does have a good reason to call for one. "I promised Mr. Headhunter, I would call this week to see if we could arrange a meeting in the next while. . . ."

ANOTHER EXAMPLE

Here is another introductory letter, this time from Jane Hopeful, an experienced teacher. Jane is applying to reenter her profession after an absence of six years taken when her two children were infants.

JANE B. HOPEFUL
2345 Desolation Road
Industry City, North America
Ph. (555) 555-5555

October 3, 19XX

Mr. Herbert Headstrong
Director of Education
Dreadnought Board of Education
Dreadnought, North America

Dear Mr. Headstrong,

Grabber

As a teacher with the Mulberry Board of Education, I set up and implemented an innovative enrichment program for gifted children. This program was well received by students and parents and has since formed the basis for similar programs throughout the system.

Transition

Since you may have need for a teacher with this kind of experience and initiative, you might be interested in other aspects of my career.

Accomplishments

—Completed an innovative teaching program at Headfull University graduating in the top 15% of my class. Program focused on individualizing instruction and design of alternative teaching methods.

—While teaching primary students at an inner city elementary school, developed an intramural physical education program for disadvantaged senior

132

students. Program led to reduced truancy and dropout rate and is still in place six years later.

—Was asked by regional teacher's association to develop and instruct a time management program for novice teachers. Program was well attended and oversubscribed on successive offerings.

—While taking a leave from active teaching to raise two active toddlers, completed three classes towards a Master's degree in Education, placing near the top of all classes.

—Pioneered experimental use of a revised reading program for an urban school system of 25,000 students. The assessment that I prepared on the program formed the basis for management's decision that the program would not be effective and thus it was not adopted system-wide, saving $250,000.

What Next?

I would like to meet with you in the near future to discuss possible openings within your system for next term. I will call you within ten days to see if it is possible to schedule an interview.

Sincerely,

Jane B. Hopeful

From reading Jane's letter, you will note that it is impossible to tell that she has not been teaching for the past six years. This would be much more difficult to disguise in a resume. Although a potential employer would undoubtedly ascertain this before offering Jane a position, there would have been time to learn many of her positive aspects, providing a balanced picture.

Jane has also been very careful to include accomplishments that focus on areas that she thinks will be important to the school system. In each case she has adhered to the checklist of points that are important in defining accomplishments.

HOW TO USE YOUR LETTER

Glen's or Jane's letters are examples of the kind of letter you should use in response to a specific advertisement or when you think that a company may have a position that is not advertised. It can also be used as a promotional letter to be mailed en masse to those firms within a certain locale you think might be interested in a person with your skills.

Very often an advertisement will request a resume and there is a natural inclination on the part of many job seekers to comply with this request. This is a mistake. *Never, under any circumstances, forward your resume as your first formal effort to get a job.* You will not be penalized for sending the type of letter just described in lieu of a resume, and you will not have provided the kind of specific information contained in a resume that could screen you out.

In order to test my hypothesis that you can get a long way in the recruiting process without using a resume, one of my clients decided to put it to the ultimate test. He applied for a professional position with a government department.

It is very usual for government recruiters to require use of a resume, sometimes requiring even a completed application form containing the same information.

Much to his surprise the job seeker made his way through

initial screening, personal interview, and progressed to a finalist position before his resume was requested. At this point it was very much to his advantage to provide the resume and he was subsequently offered the position.

It is to the employer's advantage to request a resume early in the recruiting process. It is to your advantage to ignore this request.

WHAT TO DO NEXT

After you have forwarded your letter, whether it is in response to a specific advertisement or hunch on your part, you are far from finished in your search for a job. Possibly you sent several letters to different employers at the same time. A simultaneous campaign for several jobs enhances the chances that you will have more than one offer to consider when you have worked your way through the recruiting maze. Applying for jobs successively takes too long and gives you no chance for the bargaining that can be advantageous when you are offered more than one job at the same time.

Keep copies of letters you write to each company in order to be certain that you telephone each company within the time indicated in your letter. Your phone call should be brief and to the point. Once you get through to the individual you want, you should say something like: "Mr. Headhunter, it's Glen Dollars calling. I wrote to you last week in regard to the financial services position. I was hoping that we might be able to get together in the next week or so to discuss the position and my interest in greater depth?"

One problem may be getting through the secretary or receptionist who screens Mr. Headhunter's calls. You will probably be asked, "Who shall I say is calling?" or "May I tell Mr. Headhunter what your call is about?" Your answer should be something like, "I promised Mr. Headhunter that I would call him this week in order to discuss the financial services position." If Mr. Headhunter is "busy just now," ask when it would be convenient to return the call. If the receptionist offers to have Mr. Headhunter "return your call," indicate that you are in and out of your office a great deal and that it would probably be easier for him if you call back at a convenient time.

It may be that once you have got through to Mr. Headhunter he will indicate some reason why he cannot meet personally with you just yet. Here are some common reasons and your possible responses.

1. "We're just looking at the applications right now and have not made any decisions just yet."

   Thank Mr. Headhunter. Tell him that you are anxious to discuss the position with him but that you will call back in a week—after he has had time to review his file. Make a note to return the call using the same strategy as your earlier call.

2. "If you will forward a copy of your resume, I would be very glad to read it."

   Once again thank Mr. Headhunter for his interest. Tell him that you are just preparing your resume and expect to have it ready within a few days. Ask if it would be appropriate for you to bring your resume to an interview. If Mr. Headhunter says that he wants your resume first, tell him that you will be glad to send it. Use the opportunity to ask Mr. Headhunter a bit about the position but do not be overly pushy or you will probably turn him off. Send your resume with the type of covering letter detailed in the next section.

3. "We've already made a preliminary selection on the basis of the applications received and I regret that you were not included."

   Thank Mr. Headhunter for considering your application. Tell him that, while you regret not being selected for further consideration, you wish him the best in selecting the candidate that best meets his needs. Follow this up with the type of letter detailed in the next section.

4. "We don't plan to interview many candidates. We'll be making our assessment on the basis of the resumes and

applications and will then select two or three people for personal interviews."

Thank Mr. Headhunter for considering your application. Ask him if there is other information that he would like in your case that would assist him in his decision. Provide that information if requested. Follow up with the type of letter detailed in the next section.

FOLLOW-UP LETTERS

As just described, there are other kinds of letters you will need in your job search campaign. The first is a letter you can use after a resume has been personally requested by the recruiter. The letter carries on with the example of Jane B. Hopeful, the teacher seeking a position with the Dreadnought Board of Education.

JANE B. HOPEFUL
2345 Desolation Road
Industry City, North America
Ph. (555) 555-5555

October 11, 19XX

Mr. Herbert Headstrong
Director of Education
Dreadnought Board of Education
Dreadnought, North America

Dear Mr. Headstrong,

Thank you for giving me the opportunity to discuss the elementary school teaching position with you yesterday by telephone. As I understand it, you are now completing your initial screening of candidates and would like additional information to assist you in your selection for this position.

Based on our conversation, it seems that you are looking for a thoroughly experienced elementary teacher with particular skills in program development and parental liaison.

You will note from my resume that following my education at Headfull University, which stressed innovative programming, I developed special programs for disadvantaged students and evaluated a revised reading program for two different school systems. During my short leave from teaching while raising my children, I pursued graduate work in education studying various techniques to foster school-home involvement.

I have enclosed my resume as you requested. I hope to be able to meet with you to discuss this position and will plan to call you within a week to see if this can be arranged.

Once again thank you for talking with me and describing this challenging teaching position with the Dreadnought Board of Education.

Sincerely,

Jane B. Hopeful

A different type of letter is called for when you have been told that you have not made the preliminary selection list or have not been interviewed because of your lack of qualifications or the strength of other candidates. Ms. Hopeful might write the kind of letter detailed below but would not enclose her resume.

JANE B. HOPEFUL
2345 Desolation Road
Industry City, North America
Ph. (555) 555-5555

October 11, 19XX

Mr. Herbert Headstrong
Director of Education
Dreadnought Board of Education
Dreadnought, North America

Dear Mr. Headstrong,

Thank you for giving me the opportunity to discuss the elementary school teaching position with you yesterday by telephone. As I understand it, you have now reviewed the applications and have established a short list that does not include my application.

While I am disappointed not to have been selected as a short listed candidate, I wish you the very best in selecting a candidate who best meets the needs of the Dreadnought Board of Education.

I am still very much interested in employment with your system and hope that, should you be unsuccessful in attracting the candidate that meets your needs exactly, you will reconsider my application. Should that be the case, I would be delighted to meet with you in order to outline my background and accomplishments as they pertain to the needs of your system.

Once again thank you for your consideration. I look forward to meeting with you in the future.

Sincerely,

Jane B. Hopeful

If after telephoning you are told that you are still under consideration but a resume is not specifically requested, you should write the following type of letter. Do not enclose your resume with this letter.

JANE B. HOPEFUL
2345 Desolation Road
Industry City, North America
Ph. (555) 555-5555

October 11, 19XX

Mr. Herbert Headstrong
Director of Education
Dreadnought Board of Education
Dreadnought, North America

Dear Mr. Headstrong,

Thank you for giving me the opportunity to discuss the elementary school teaching position with you yesterday by telephone. As I understand it, you are now completing your initial screening of candidates for this position and will be establishing a short list before conducting personal interviews.

Based on our conversation, I understand that you are looking for a thoroughly experienced elementary teacher with particular skills in program development and parental liaison.

As I mentioned during our brief telephone conversation, following my education at Headfull University, which stressed innovative programming, I developed special programs for disadvantaged students and evaluated a revised reading program for two different school systems. During my short leave from teaching while raising my children, I pursued graduate work in education studying various techniques to foster school—home involvement.

I hope to meet with you to discuss this position once you have established a list of candidates you wish to interview. I will call you within a week to see if this can be arranged.

Once again thank you for talking with me and describing this challenging teaching position with the Dreadnought Board of Education.

Sincerely,

Jane B. Hopeful

Chapter 12

Resumes

"The best liar is he who makes the smallest amount of lying go the longest way."
—*The Way of All Flesh* by Samuel Butler.

Good letters are the most important written part of your job search campaign. Used consistently as the first step and even the second step after a phone conversation, they will yield a greater number of personal interviews than a resume. But you will still need a first-rate resume to increase the likelihood that you will actually get the job you want.

Although I have said that resumes are overrated and overused, they are undeniably a crucial part of the job search process if for no other reason than everybody expects you to have one. But most resumes do not do the job they are intended to do— sell you to the employer.

Let us look at an example of a typical resume and the accompanying letter that might be sent in response to an advertisement for a technical professional position. In fact both the letter and the resume are better than many that cross most recruiters' desks and would be considered highly professional by typical white-collar job seekers.

POLYMER
RESEARCH
CORPORATION

Exciting Career Opportunity

RESEARCH ENGINEER—PLASTICS DIVISION

Reporting to the Managing Engineer—Plastics Division, this position will appeal to the experienced and creative individual who thrives on exercising a great deal of individual authority and initiative.

Initially the successful applicant will be assigned to the Apollo Plastics Project developing new synthetic materials for a government sponsored high technology venture. Supervisory responsibilities for junior technical personnel will also be required. You will be part of a dynamic team that works hard and enjoys it.

If you are a thoroughly experienced engineer with a wealth of experience in plastics and would like to be part of this exciting team, call or write in confidence to:

Director of Professional Recruiting
Polymer Research Corporation
2345 DeGrande Avenue
Industry City, North America
Ph. (555) 555-1111

JAMES B. HOPEFUL
2345 Desolation Road
Industry City, North America
Ph. (555) 555-5555

September 21, 19XX

Director of Professional Recruiting
Polymer Research Corporation
2345 DeGrande Avenue
Industry City, North America

Dear Sir,

In response to your advertisement in the Industry City Crier of September 20, 19XX for a Research Engineer: Plastics Division, I enclose my resume for your consideration.

You will note from my resume that I have ten years direct experience in chemical research as well as completed a Ph.D. in Chemical Engineering from Hotshot University. I have excellent organizational and supervisory skills, and pride myself on a creative attitude toward my work.

You will note from my resume that I have worked directly in the plastics field and I believe my experience in petrochemical by-products is directly applicable to this position as well. I would appreciate the opportunity of discussing this position further with you.

I would like to meet with you in order to discuss this position and may be reached at 555-5555.

I look forward to hearing from you.

Sincerely,

James B. Hopeful

Resume

JAMES B. HOPEFUL
2345 Desolation Road
Industry City, North America
Phone: (555) 555-5555

Career Goals

I hope to progress to positions that will allow me a broad administrative scope as well as satisfy my research interests. In the longer term I would hope to direct major research projects including technical and personnel responsibilities.

Education

Ph.D. (19XX) from Hotshot University with research work in crystalline structures of synthetic artichokes. B.Sc. (19XX) and M.Sc. (19XX) in Chemical Engineering from Not–so–Hotshot University. Several research papers published.

Personal

Age 34, married with three children; wife (Jane) is successful architect. Hobbies include nonfiction reading, mountain climbing, botany, and amateur photography.

Experience

June 19XX–Present

Amalgamated Fortune 500 Corporation, Workcity, Anystate. Research Chemist in charge of Synthetic Artichoke Division. Job responsibilities include budgeting, directing staff of two technicians, and development of contract research proposals. Reason for Leaving: Seeking greater opportunity.

March 19XX–June 19XX

Synthetic Developments Corporation, Workcity, Anystate. Laboratory Research Chemist in Engineering Division of major plastics manufacturer. Assigned job responsibilities included evaluating proposed plastics manufacturing processes and quality control of specialized production.
Reason for Leaving: Company lost government contract.

September 19XX–December 19XX

DegreeMill University, Workcity, Anystate. Laboratory Assistant working on petrochemical by-product research. Duties included complex experimentation and laboratory maintenance.
Reason for Leaving: Obtained more senior position elsewhere.

March 19XX–December 19XX

Xenephonic International, Workcity, Anystate. Laboratory Technician in commercial laboratory specializing in synthetic duck feathers. Major areas of responsibility included laboratory maintenance, materials ordering, and basic experimentation.
Reason for Leaving: Seeking more responsibility.

Summer Employment 19XX–19XX

During eight different summers I have held positions as hotel busboy, taxi driver, delivery man, construction laborer, laboratory maintenance technician, and groundskeeper. Each position was full time during the summer and several carried on part-time during the college year.

References

Mr. Dayton Argyle, Senior Researcher
Synthetic Development Corporation
1234 Cheshire Street
Workcity, Anystate
Ph. (555) 222-2222

Dr. Fred Brainscan, Research Fellow
DegreeMill University
4321 Knowledge Avenue
Workcity, Anystate
Ph. (555) 333-3333

Rev. Allan Divine
54321 Prayer Avenue
Industry City, North America
Ph. (555) 444-4444

References from my current employer are confidential but available on request.

Mr. Hopeful has told the careful reader:

1. What he wants out of life.
2. That he had the patience to educate himself for a long time.
3. That he has been successful in siring progeny and has a number of other recreational pursuits.
4. That a number of organizations have hired him for a variety of duties.
5. That several people will speak well of him if requested to do so.

The letter and resume you have just read provide the basic information available to the recruiter about most candidates. As I said before, this letter and resume are better than most that cross recruiters' desks simply because they are short and concise. However, they do not come close to doing justice to Mr. Hopeful's abilities.

The typical resume and letter used in the job search process reads like a job description—it lists all of the things you were supposed to do and where you were supposed to have done them.

Your resume should maintain the same principles that you have already used in the letter-writing portion of your job search campaign. It should highlight your accomplishments in very specific ways, discount or disguise negative information, and be an inducement for the recruiter to continue exploring your application. Be aware that you will probably not get a job solely as a result of a good resume, but a poor resume can prevent you from getting one.

There are several principles to keep in mind in writing a good resume:

1. Keep It Short

Your resume should be no longer than two pages. Whatever its length, it will be scanned in fifteen to forty-five seconds and you hinder your case by including more information than the reader can assimilate in that time.

A common mistake made by many resume writers is including too much information in the hope that something will rouse a reader's interest. Do not include too many details—even if these reflect positively on your case. Get in, make a strong general impression, and get out.

2. Organize the Information

Headings and format are important in doing this. When you finish, let someone else read your resume—once—and see how much they can remember.

3. Keep It Specific

Do not try to cover every possible job with one resume. For example, if you are an engineer applying for jobs that range from middle management to design, you will need more than one resume. Each resume can highlight only those aspects of your background that are appropriate for the type of position you are seeking.

4. Accentuate the Positive

Ignore or discount negative information about yourself in the resume. If you think you are too old or young, do not include your age. If you have been fired, do not mention it. If you have been a job-hopper, do not list your jobs chronologically.

5. Manage the Reader's Inferences

Remember that the most important thing you want to accomplish is to have the reader form positive inferences about your ability as a result of reading your resume. They will not form those inferences by reading your previous job descriptions, but they might if you show them what you have accomplished—what you can do.

The most important part of your resume is the beginning. In fact, if the reader took your resume, tore the first page in half horizontally, and retained only the top half of the first page, the important information about you should be available.

Aside from the usual demographic information, the first half of page one should contain a section entitled *Career Highlights*. It is important because, like your action letter, it summarizes what you have done. Your highlights say, "If you remember nothing else about me, remember this. . . ." Here are two examples from individuals you have already read about in *CareerScan*. The first one is done in traditional prose style, the second in point form. Depending on your highlights and intended audience, either is acceptable.

Career Highlights: Set up and implemented innovative enrichment program for gifted children that has formed the basis for similar programs throughout Whizbang Board of Education. Pioneered use of revised reading program in urban school system of 2,500 students. Developed extracurricular program for disadvantaged students at inner-city high school. Completed model teacher education program specializing in individualized instruction graduating in top 15% of class. Completed Master's degree in Education graduating near top of class while raising two toddlers. Developed well received teacher in-service program for regional Teacher's Association.

Career Highlights: Developed wide-ranging financial reporting and management systems spanning four major North American corporations that have stood the test of time.

— Designed and used a new performance appraisal system for management employees of major bank
— Wrote two major articles on financial reporting systems published by major international magazines.
— Utilized novel takeover procedures to successfully procure assets of competitor.
— Developed plan for use of microcomputers for multi-branch financial management offices

— Completed graduate degree in business receiving major graduate award for research on financial modeling systems. Completed grueling executive self-development program
— Developed innovative legacy program for major university, increasing donations by 12%
— Pioneered an executives-in-training program for major international oil company

Writing Your Own Career Highlights

It is now time for you to begin writing your own Career Highlights section of your resume. Refer to your accomplishments but do not copy them exactly. Use action verbs but summarize and make your accomplishments more pointed.

_____

_____

_____

_____

_____

_____

_____

_____

_____

_____

THE REST OF YOUR RESUME

If you write a good Career Highlights section, you are well underway to producing a good resume. Like your highlights, the rest of your resume points out what you have accomplished while at the same time providing descriptive information about your background.

Here are some specific do's and don't's for the balance of your resume.

1. Do not include months when citing the dates you were employed at each company. Including only years can help disguise short interruptions in your background as well as reducing the amount of irrelevant information provided to the recruiter.

2. Do include one or two accomplishments under each job. Make sure that these accomplishments are different from those you have already used in your Career Highlights. If you are including accomplishments already used in your action letter—and you probably should—rephrase them slightly.

3. Do not refer to your job description when writing your resume. Focus on what you did—not what you were supposed to have done.

4. If you are listing your jobs chronologically, start with your current position. If you are listing your experience by skill area rather than employer (see resume example 2, page 147), put your most marketable skill area first.

5. Include the first name and telephone number of the references you decide to use in your resume. In using references be sure to ask beforehand. A good question to ask potential references is, "Would you feel comfortable giving me a good reference?" If they are reluctant or noncommittal, use somebody else. You should provide three references. At least two of these should be past employers who can speak knowledgeably about your

performance. If you have grave doubts about the reliability of a reference, either select somebody else or have a friend phone for a reference on you for a fictitious recruiter.

6. Do not include reasons for having done anything. Most particularly do not include information about why you left or would like to leave previous or current employers.

7. Do include special information about yourself that makes you marketable. Languages spoken or written, foreign service, unusual experience—all serve to raise you one cut above the crowd. This could either be included in a section entitled "Special Skills & Interests" or integrated with other areas.

Here are two examples of resumes. The first one uses a traditional accomplishment-based chronological style. The second one is functional; it provides information by groups of accomplishments. In each instance we are dealing with Jane Hopeful, our teacher attempting to pursue her career after a lapse of six years.

Personal Resume

Name: JANE B. HOPEFUL

Address: 2345 Desolation Road
            Industry City, North America

Phone: Ph. (555) 555-5555

Career Highlights: Set up and implemented in-novative enrichment program for gifted children that has formed the basis for similar programs throughout Whizbang Board of Education. Pioneered experimental use of innovative reading program in urban school system of 2,500 students. Developed innovative extracurricular program for disadvan-taged students at inner-city high school. Graduat-ing in top 15% of class, completed innovative teacher education program specializing in indi-vidualized instruction. Completed Master's degree in Education graduating near top of class while raising two toddlers. Developed well received teacher in-service program for regional Teacher's Association.

Education: Completed innovative B. Ed. (19XX) degree at Headfull University. Program focused on individualizing instruction and design of alterna-tive teaching methods. Completed two thirds of coursework for Master's degree in Education, fin-ishing each class in top third.

Professional Background:

Mulberry Board of Education, Mulberry, North America

19XX–19XX   As Elementary School Teacher instructing grades three and four in a large inner-city elementary school, developed innovative intramural physical education program for low achieving senior students. Program led to reduced truancy and dropout rate. Carried classload of thirty-two students including two with severe learning handicaps. Received very favorable ratings from local superintendents for reading skill program developed over a two-year period. Active as coach for junior basketball team involving seventy students over three years.

Whizbang Board of Education, Whizbang, North America

19XX–19XX   As Primary Teacher and Language Arts Resource Teacher for senior students, developed a comprehensive reading program for a school of 1,800 students. This program formed the basis for system-wide changes in reading programs. As extra project developed and managed in-service program on time management for novice teachers. Organized and managed annual district field meet, developing new eliminations procedure that saved 25% of usual time. Received commendation from local parents' group for class project on family relationships.

<u>Mindblow District Education Board,</u> Mindblow, North
America

19XX–19XX   As Itinerant Language Arts Teacher for
three urban schools, pioneered use of
revised reading program for system of
25,000 students. Prepared report that
formed the basis of system's decision
not to adopt the revised program. Instructed language arts to seventy-
eight senior students, maintaining
truancy rate below system average. Developed student–consultant program
for senior students tutoring low-
achieving juniors. Program has developed into a system model.

<u>Summer and Part–Time Employment</u> (Various
Employers)

19XX–19XX   Completed camp counsellor training
program specializing in handicapped
children. Subsequently worked three
summers in two camps for 12– to 14–
year–old children. Managed one camp
for last half of one summer. Drove taxi
in large urban center part–time during
college.

<u>Additional Information</u>
    Area representative for professional
teachers' association for three
years. Member of local symphony board
of directors in charge of young talent
program.

<u>Special Skills & Interests</u>
    Fluent in written and conversational
Spanish and French. Speak several
other languages at tourist level of
proficiency.

References

Mr. D. W. (Darryl) Superstar
Director of Instruction
Mulberry Board of Education
Mulberry, North America
Ph. (555) 555-5555

Mrs. H. H. (Hanna) Priceless
Curriculum Superintendent
Whizbang Board of Education
Whizbang, North America
Ph. (555) 555-5555

Prof. J. L. (Jason) Dullspeak
Headfull University
College Town, North America
Ph. (555) 555-5555 (Ex. 55)

Personal Resume

Name: JANE B. HOPEFUL

Address: 2345 Desolation Road
             Industry City, North America

Phone: Ph. (555)555-5555

Career Highlights: Set up and implemented innovative enrichment program for gifted children
that has formed the basis for similar programs
throughout Whizbang Board of Education. Pioneered
use of innovative reading program in urban school
system of 2,500 students. Developed innovative extracurricular program for disadvantaged students
at inner—city high school. Completed innovative
teacher education program specializing in indi-
vidualized instruction graduating in top 15% of
class. Completed Master's degree in Education
graduating near top of class while raising two
toddlers. Developed well received teacher in-
service program for regional Teacher's
Association.

Education: Completed innovative B. Ed. (19XX)
degree from Headfull University. Program focused
on individualizing instruction and design of alternative teaching methods. Completed two thirds
of coursework for Master's degree in Education,
finishing each class in top third.

Professional Background

Program Development: As an Elementary School
Teacher for grades three and four children in Mulberry, North America, developed innovative intra—

mural program for low achieving senior students at an inner-city elementary school. Program led to reduced truancy and dropout rates. While employed by Whizbang Board of Education from 19XX-19XX, developed comprehensive reading program for a school of 1,800 students. This program formed the basis of system-wide changes in reading programs. Received commendation from local parents' group for class project on family relationships. Developed and managed in-service program on time management for novice teachers.

Instruction: Carried classload of thirty-two students including two with severe learning handicaps while employed as teacher grades three and four at Mulberry Board of Education. Received very favorable ratings from local superintendents for reading skill program developed and taught over a two-year period. While employed by Whizbang Board of Education as Primary Teacher and Language Arts Resource Teacher for senior students, instructed students across all grades. As Itinerant Languages Teacher for Mindblow District Education Board, pioneered instructional use of a new reading program. My report formed basis of system's decision not to adopt program. Instructed three summers in camp setting for 12- to 14-year-old handicapped children. Instructed language arts to 78 senior students in inner-city elementary school, maintaining truancy rate below system average.

Extra Curricular: Active as coach for junior basketball team while employed for three years by the Mulberry Board of Education. Handled 70 students over three years. Organized and managed annual district field meet for schools of the Whizbang Board of Education. Developed new eliminations procedure that saved 25% of usual time. Developed student-consultant program for senior students tutoring low-achieving juniors while employed as Itinerant Languages Teacher by Mindblow District Education Board. Program has developed into a system model. Completed camp counsellor training program specializing in handicapped children.

Additional Information
Area representative for professional teachers' association for three years. Member of local symphony board of directors in charge of young talent program.

Special Skills & Interests
Fluent in written and conversational Spanish and French. Speak several other languages at tourist level of proficiency.

References

Mr. D. W. (Darryl) Superstar
Director of Instruction
Mulberry Board of Education
Mulberry, North America
Ph. (555)555-5555

Mrs. H. H. (Hanna) Priceless
Curriculum Superintendent
Whizbang Board of Education
Whizbang, North America
Ph. (555)555-5555

Prof. J. L. (Jason) Dullspeak
Headfull University
College Town, North America
Ph. (555)555-5555 (Ex. 55)

WRITING YOUR OWN RESUME

You are now at the point where you should be able to write your own resume. The first things to decide are the style of resume you will use and the type of potential position you want to target. Remember that you cannot properly construct a resume that will portray you as all things to all people. The best resume is one that is short and that details only the aspects important for the type of job you are seeking. In most instances the chronological-accomplishments–based resume (example 1, page 156) is the most acceptable one to use. The functional resume (example 2, page 160) is most useful when you want to hide or disguise certain information, such as Jane Hopeful's six-year absence from teaching.

Write your resume, adding the chronological, educational, and reference information to the highlights you have already composed. Be wary of returning to a style that simply lists your job functions when detailing your experience in each position. One example is worth many lists!

USING YOUR RESUME

You already know what *not to do* with your resume; that is, send it out willy-nilly to prospective employers or send it in response to an advertised job vacancy. But where and how should you use it?

The ideal time to hand out your resume is after you have had a personal interview. It then serves as a summary of your interview and is read with more of a positive orientation than it would be if the interviewer had seen it too soon. Unfortunately it is not always possible to wait. Sometimes you must surrender your resume before you would like simply to avoid offending the recruiter.

Only surrender your personal resume when someone asks you pointblank for it—over the phone or in a personal interview. Like the army, do not volunteer!

Bob was a senior accountant employed by a major urban shopping center. After five years in this job he had applied for a controller's position with a multibranch specialty foods franchise.

Bob used an accomplishment-based action-letter in making his initial inquiry for the controller's position. This resulted in a call from a vice president of the company with a request for a resume.

As a result of this call, Bob was able to ascertain that one key factor in the new job would be familiarity with computerized systems and profit-center operating procedures. Although he had only a modest amount of experience in this area, even that was detailed very little in his prepared resume.

By waiting Bob was able to obtain information vital to editing his resume. Thus he was able to rework his accomplishments to demonstrate expertise in areas the vice president had noted as important before he forwarded his resume. Subsequently he obtained an interview and was offered the job.

Copy your resume onto high quality rag paper using a professional photocopying or Xerox process. If you have access to a word processor, send originals each time. Do not print a great number of copies because you will probably want to change something in the original to meet the demands of a specific opportunity. Do not include a photograph—unless you are a great deal better looking than you think you are.

Written well and used properly, your resume can be a powerful ally in your search for a job. Unlike traditional resumes, yours can tell a prospective employer why you should be hired—rather than providing justifications to discard your application.

Chapter 13

The Interview

". . . the excruciating process during which personnel officers separate the wheat from the chaff—and then hire the chaff."—*Buzzwords* by J. Fisk and R. Barron

No matter how impressive you sound on paper, you are unlikely to be offered a job on the basis of your written information alone. At best you will be able to gauge the success of your written job search campaign by the number of personal interviews you are able to obtain. Interviews will determine your ultimate success in getting the job you want.

A good written job search campaign yields interviews. A good interview yields job offers.

There are several important points to keep in mind about interviews, whether these interviews are being conducted by telephone or in person.

1. Don't forget the interviewer.
The cardinal rule of being interviewed is "Do not make the interviewer feel bad (foolish, dumb, put-down, anxious) as a result of talking to you." If you can do nothing else, make certain that interviewing you is not threatening to the interviewer. This is especially important in dealing with an

unskilled interviewer, one who may feel more ill-at-ease than you do.

You accomplish this by answering questions that you are asked, speaking long enough (but not too long) in response to questions so that the interviewer can formulate the next question, and by appearing interested in what the interviewer has to say. Very few questions call for a yes or no answer and those that do should probably be dodged.

2. Think—then—talk.

Your major task in being interviewed is to *organize* your personal information so that the interviewer will remember it. After the interview the interviewer will remember only a few key facts about you and you want to ensure that important information is remembered.

We will deal later with how you can organize answers to specific important questions you are likely to be asked during a telephone or personal interview. A general rule of thumb is to mentally prepare yourself in advance for standard questions so that rather than formulating your answer when asked, you need only remember what you decided to answer. This does not mean that you must memorize canned responses to questions, but you should have at least a general idea of what you will say and how you will say it when you are asked typical questions in an interview. You should never approach an interview saying to yourself, "I hope they don't ask me. . . ." Assume that you will be asked and prepare for it.

3. Remember what you are selling.

In answering questions you should provide support for positive things you are saying about yourself. This means that you should not speak in an overly general manner about something but rather try to find an opportunity to use one of your specific accomplishments to bolster a point you are trying to make. The interviewer will remember the specific example or accomplishment long after the generality has been forgotten.

If you are asked about your experience in a certain area, do not simply itemize what you have done. Detailing one or two accomplishments in a format similar to what you have already been doing in your written information will give the interviewer something to remember. It does no good to tell an interviewer that you are a certain type of individual (experienced, creative, honest, etc.)—that is heard so often it is not believed. Focus on what you have accomplished— this forms a base the interviewer will use to make a positive inference about you.

4. Do not piddle in your own tent.

Do not volunteer negative information about yourself to the interviewer and if you must talk about a weakness do so in a manner that downplays or discounts its importance.

Do not talk about what you have not done or use words like *just* or *only* to describe your experience in an area. If asked directly about your experience in a "soft" area, indicate what you have done that is as close as possible to the desirable area and support this with an accomplishment. Refer to examples given later in *CareerSpan* for possible responses to typical questions.

5. Put on your ears.

Listen to what the interviewer is saying and be certain that you understand questions you are asked.

A common mistake made by job seekers is listening only to enough of a question to trigger a response on their part. They then answer the question they thought was asked. If you are not certain about what is intended by a question, do not simply guess and answer—ask. You might say something like, "I'm not certain about what you mean. Do you mean X or Y?" You could also paraphrase the question to be certain that you understand the meaning—"You would like to know if I have hands-on experience in operational areas. . . ?"

6. Do not steal the baton.

Deal with issues and questions in the sequence dictated by the interviewer. If you have questions you would like to have answered, wait until the end of the interview or until you are asked. Let the interviewer set the pace and style of the interview unless you are particularly adroit at doing this unnoticed.

THE TELEPHONE INTERVIEW

In most cases you will be assessed by a short formal telephone interview before you are asked for a personal interview. Although actual practice differs from company to company, this kind of contact is often used to gain a bit more information about you or to see if you impress as well in conversation as you already have by letter. This telephone interview may not sound like an interview at all—perhaps only a request for answers to a few questions—but it is important to do well. Then chances are that you will be asked to appear for a personal interview. If not, you will be thanked politely for the information and receive your "Dear John Archer" letter in due course.

If you are called by a prospective employer at an inopportune moment or caught off guard by the call, do not be afraid to tell the caller that you are tied up just now and offer to call back (or request a call back) at a specified time. This is much better than going ahead with the interview and doing poorly because you are not ready. Use the additional time to reacquaint yourself with the prospective job.

Be prepared to answer specific questions that center on the accomplishments you cited in your introductory action letter. Do not forget what information you supplied. It is pretty embarrassing to have to ask the caller for more information about one of your accomplishments before you can describe it in greater detail!

When you are asked by the caller for more information, do not revert to listing or reciting the additionally requested information. Carry on with your example-based specific approach. Providing additional information on one accomplishment often gives you the chance to document another accomplishment at the same time. If Jane Hopeful, our prospective teacher, is asked for additional information on the enrichment program she started with the Whizbang Board of Education, she can answer the specific question and then say that this was similar to another program she initiated with another school system and then go on to describe that program. Never miss an opportunity to introduce specific examples of what you have accomplished.

In citing additional accomplishments during a telephone interview, one good example is better than one good one and three half-good ones.

Do not expect that the telephone interview will give you the opportunity to describe your background fully. Nor will it provide you with all the information you might require about a job. The best you can hope for is to find out a bit more about the job so that you will be able to tailor your resume to fit the specific attributes they are looking for.

During the telephone interview, do not ask questions that could prejudice your chances of getting the job. This would include questions about salary or other benefits, working conditions, future career prospects, or any other area that would look self-serving. You may be asked if you have any questions. In that case a good type of question to ask is "Could you tell me how this position relates to the xxx position?" or, "What personal characteristic would be most beneficial in the person who can best do the job for you?" If you have no questions when you are asked, do not simply say no. Say, "I had wondered about xxx but you have already given me all the information I need in that area."

If it looks like the telephone conversation will be terminated without an invitation for personal interview being extended to you, do not simply thank the caller and hang up. Ask a question that will tell you about the disposition of your application. You might say something like, "I want to thank you for calling me in order to obtain more information. What is the next step in your recruiting campaign? When do you expect to be able to schedule personal interviews?" Close the conversation by reiterating your interest in the position and indicating that you look forward to meeting the caller when personal interviews are arranged.

If you are not asked for a personal interview during your telephone conversation, do not despair. Sometimes an employer is not in a position to make such an offer during your telephone interview. The caller may simply want to gather more information before making a decision about whether or not to talk personally with you.

Whether or not you have not been offered a personal interview as a result of your telephone interview, be sure to write a follow-up letter. This letter should reinforce points raised in your telephone interview as a prelude to a personal interview or it can act as an additional incentive for the employer to schedule a personal interview in the near future. If your personal interview is scheduled in close proximity to your telephone interview and some distance is involved, you may wish to send this letter via express mail. It is expensive but worth it.

Such a letter is concise but gives you the opportunity to introduce an accomplishment specifically targeted to your enhanced knowledge of the job requirements. Here is an example based on Glen B. Dollars, the financial services manager described earlier who is seeking new career opportunities.

Glen R. Dollars
12445 Hopeful Road
Finance, North America
Ph. (555) 555-5555

November 14, 19XX

Mr. Head Hunter
Global Executive Recruiting Ltd.
12345 Pathos Blvd.
Opportunity City, North America

Dear Mr. Hunter:

Thank you for calling me today to discuss my interest in the Financial Services Manager position you
are staffing for a major North American food whole-
saler. I appreciated the opportunity to gain additional information about Consolidated Foodstuffs
and the progress of my application for this senior
position.

As I understand it, you are looking for a thoroughly
experienced financial professional with strength
in computerized applications, particularly inventory management. An additional requirement is the
ability to deal effectively with a team of nonfinancial professionals in translating organizational
requirements into economically viable corporate
operating policies.

As I noted in our brief conversation, these requirements are similar in scope and level of responsibility to my position as Manager of Financial Services
for the Third National Bank of Destitution. In that
position I was able to design complicated financial
takeover procedures for a major competitor—and
convince a group of nonfinancial professionals of
the viability of my novel approach. And while em-

ployed as a Financial Manager for a multinational petroleum corporation, I developed an improved inventory system for petrochemical by-products resulting in sizeable savings.

[I look forward to meeting with you on Friday, November 27, at 2:30 P.M. to further discuss my candidacy for this position.]
(or)
[I look forward to hearing from you again when you have established your schedule for personal interviews.]

Once again thank you for extending to me the courtesy of a telephone interview. I look forward to meeting with you soon.

Personally,

Glen R. Dollars

THE PERSONAL INTERVIEW

The personal interview is the goal you have worked for in your job search quest. It is what will determine if you get the job—or if it will be given to a competitor.

In traveling to your interview, allow yourself sufficient lead time to account for unplanned delays. A flat tire or missed plane connection may be understandable but it is better to have those accidents after you are already employed. Arrive three to five minutes in advance of your appointment.

There has been much written about personal decorum in interviews. Simply put, you should look, act, and smell like a professional, like someone you would want to work for you if you were doing the recruiting. A well pressed conservative business suit and polished shoes (male or female), clean teeth, fresh breath, well groomed hair, and effective deodorant are essential. If you use cologne, aftershave, or perfume, err on the side of understatement. If inclined toward flatulence, watch your diet.

Appearance probably will not win you many points no matter what you do, but you could stand to lose a great deal if you violate popular convention.

Prepare for your interview by finding out as much as possible about your prospective employer. Annual reports or other publicly available written information is useful for researching corporations or public institutions but, for really useful information, nothing beats an insider. You may have a friend or a friend may have a friend who either works for or knows your prospective employer well. Your professional association can prove invaluable in locating a colleague who may be willing to provide additional useful information.

Try to find out about the interpersonal atmosphere of the employer, who influences who, what things are sensitive, or what they are really looking for in a prospective candidate. Do not be too forward in obtaining this information unless you are

173

certain of the confidence of your insider. Otherwise be satisfied with information that is more than public but less than private.

Review all of your accomplishments in advance of your personal interview. You may be able to use the information you obtained from your public and private sources to tailor your accomplishments for maximum impact during your interview, perhaps using certain key words that have a special significance for your employer. Try to imagine additional questions the recruiter might ask as a follow-up to your accomplishments and be certain that you are comfortable with your intended responses. Remember that you should be able to verbally tie one accomplishment to another to ensure that you can present your key points even if you are not asked specifically about one or more areas you think are important for the job.

Ideally, the recruiter will not have an advance copy of your resume so be certain that you bring one with you to the interview. If you have some doubts about the exact description of the position, for example if you are uncertain whether it requires that you design or supervise others who design, you should prepare two resumes. Each one should favor one interpretation of the position and present your accomplishments demonstrating different skills.

If you have avoided giving the recruiter your resume until the interview, try to hold off leaving a copy until the interview is over. This will forestall the interviewer from reading your resume while you talk instead of listening to you. A good way to do this is to take the initiative. After you have been introduced to the interviewer but before you are asked specific interview questions, say something like, "I've brought a copy of my resume for you. I'd like to leave it with you after the interview as a summary of the key points we discuss." If a resume is still requested before the interview, provide one immediately so as not to prejudice your case. If you have prepared more than one resume, bring copies of each with you and leave the one that best meets your enhanced knowledge of the position gained as a result of the interview.

When you are shown in to your appointment or met by your interviewer, extend your hand for a firm businesslike handshake. Sit down where and when you are told to by the cues of the interviewer. Adopt a relaxed posture but do not slouch. Look at the interviewer throughout the interview and try to convey an air of interest and attentiveness. Do not smoke unless the interviewer does so first even if ashtrays are in sight. If you do smoke, restrict yourself to one in an hour interview.

Making the Most of Interview Questions

I have already made the point that you must organize the information that you present to the interviewer. But that is so essential that I want to repeat it. It is more important to ensure that the interviewer remember a few key points than it is for you to tell everything that you want the interviewer to hear.

If you present information about yourself piecemeal, with little attempt made to provide "memory crutches" for the interviewer, few important facts will be retained no matter how important you think they are. Even if the interviewer makes extensive notes, these are seldom used after the interview and are sometimes only random musings to ensure that sleep does not win out over interviewing.

It is impossible to underestimate the ability of the average interviewer to remember important information about you.

There are several things you can do to organize the information you provide to an interviewer to ensure remembering.

1. Key Points Are Important

Be certain that you know the key point(s) you want to convey in response to a question you are answering. If you do not know where you are going, it is unlikely the interviewer will. Highlight important statements by prefacing them with, "The most important thing about . . ." or "The major activity that I did was. . . ." This is similar to the use of underlining or highlighting while studying and alerts the reader that the following statement is important.

175

2. Remember Examples

Use an example or accomplishment to bolster a statement. Thus far I have encouraged you to use accomplishments to enhance the believability of what you are saying. Additionally, accomplishments assist the listener in remembering what he has heard. In memory the general point is tied by association to the specific example and the example is usually remembered because it is unique.

For example in answering a question about your experience in a certain area do not simply itemize what you have done if you expect it to be remembered. Tie your experience to a specific accomplishment.

3. Forget the Irrelevant

Screen out irrelevant information—even if you are tempted to keep talking because of nervousness. Be particularly wary of including trivial information too close to key points.

4. Doing Double Duty

Try to introduce a key point(s) in more than one way and at more than one point in the interview. For example if it appears that a major criterion for the job is the ability to delegate effectively do not simply bring this up at one point and then forget it. Use other accomplishments at different points in the interview that demonstrate the same skill. For instance an accomplishment dealing with supervisory style or achievement orientation can also be tied to the use of effective delegation to show your style.

5. Organize Your Answers

Provide advance organizers to the interviewer for major questions. These are analogous to headings in a book and give the listener something to look forward to. For example in response to a question about what you feel is important in supervising staff you could start your answer with, "There are three major things that I've found important. . . ." This alerts the listener to what is coming and provides advance organization to facilitate memory.

6. Summarize

Summarize your key points for major questions or those questions that necessitate extensive answers. This is the opposite of an advance organizer. It reminds the inter- viewer what was important and serves as an effective cue that you have finished answering the question (time to wake up and ask another question!). For instance in answering a question about experience you could conclude by saying, "So my experience has involved xxx and xxx and xxx."

Open and Closed Questions

You will be asked two different types of questions during your interview. The first type can be called closed questions. Closed questions are ones where a yes or no or other simple answer is expected. This would include questions about your job title with a certain employer, how many subordinates you have supervised, or whether or not you have a specific professional designation.

Specific information is requested by the interviewer who asks a closed question. You are expected to answer the question directly with little fanfare. This does not mean that you must say simply yes or no, but be wary of going on at length unless the interviewer gives you other cues that this is expected. Such cues may be head nodding, words like uh-huh or yes with an inflection that indicates you are to go on.

Open questions are another matter. An interviewer will ask open questions with the clear expectation that you are to interpret the question in your own frame of reference and answer it as you see fit. Questions that begin with "Tell me a bit about . . ." "What do you think about . . ." or "What have you done in . . ." are open. Answering an open question is more difficult than answering a closed question but it does provide you with the best opportunity to make use of your accomplishments.

The most critical thing in answering an open question is to be certain that you do not mistake it for a closed one. It is disconcerting for the interviewer to ask a question like "Tell me about your likes and dislikes in a supervisor," and to have someone reply, "I can get along with any kind of supervisor." Such a reply will catch the interviewer unaware since additional time will probably be necessary for the interviewer to think of another question to fill the silence!

If you are totally uncertain about what is meant by a question you are asked, get some clarification before you answer. Some questions are deliberately asked in a vague or general manner whereas others may appear to be asked that way because of the ineptitude of the interviewer or your listening abilities. One way to get clarification is to say something like, "I'm not certain I know what you mean. Do you mean xx or yy?" Once you get clarification—or find out that you are not going to get any— answer the open question as best you can. Keep in mind the points you have already read in this chapter, particularly with regard to use of your accomplishments in answering interview questions.

Chapter 14

Interview Questions

"The questions and answers of an interview are merely the tools used to make an evaluation, the trees in the forest of impression. Your relaxation, your confidence in yourself, and your manner are far more important than the words you use in your answers."—*Sweaty Palms* by Anthony Medley

There are some questions that are asked in nearly all personal interviews. This does not mean these are particularly good questions. Sometimes the interviewer already has the answer in written form but asks the question anyway, seemingly to fill in time.

SELLING YOUR EXPERIENCE

The most popular question is undoubtedly some variation of, "Give me a brief rundown of your experience. . . ." It is usually asked as an open question rather than a series of more specific closed ones and provides you with the single best opportunity to sell yourself to the interviewer. Unfortunately most people do not answer this question very well. Usually their answer resembles an unwelcome wander down the memory lane of work—about as interesting to listen to as someone else's weekly grocery list.

When you are asked this kind of question, reflect for a minute about what the interviewer really wants to know (or should want to know) and how your answer will be treated. What opportunities are there for you to influence the hire-or-not decision that will ultimately be made by the interviewer? The reason the interviewer asks this question is to amass the information that will be used to form crucial inferences about you. Of itself where you have worked, who you have worked with, and what you have done is meaningless to the listener. Such information acquires meaning only after the listener has used it for making inferences about your abilities and how you would be expected to perform in a different job.

Most job seekers answer this question using the chronological approach starting with their most recent position. They list their jobs and job responsibilities, ofttimes repeating the same information contained in their inadequate resumes. It is boring, so boring in fact that most interviewers often do not even bother to listen to the answer to this question, figuring that they will be able to pick up on the information when or if they read the resume.

Usually this question is poorly answered because interviewees don't understand why it was asked and are not sure how their answer can be organized for maximum impact. Most interviewees do not know what inferences they want to have formed in the mind of the interviewer. They go through the motions of being interviewed, throwing away the best opportunity they will have to sell themselves.

Using the groundwork you did for writing action letters and your resume, you can make maximum use of this opportunity. The way to answer this sort of question is to downplay the chronological approach and concentrate on the skills or abilities you have demonstrated through your experience—skills and abilities that cut across the various jobs you have persued.

Jack Waters, who has held a variety of stockbroker positions over a period of fifteen years, might begin an answer to a question about experience with, "Over the past fifteen years, I've worked for four brokerage and securities houses ranging from the branch office of a national firm to the main office of a successful regional firm. During that time, I've concentrated on three major areas.

"The most important area has been in direct sales of board listed securities to a wide ranging client group. This was the major aspect of my job as a broker with Windfall Securities in Speculative City for three years where I was able to maintain a sales record in the top 10 percent of the company over a period of three years, selling mainly to a junior professional clientele. During my four years with the Legalized Gambling Group in Investors Haven, I carried on this role, although this time specializing in junior energy stocks with an older, very affluent client group. I brought thirty new juniors on stream during that period, increasing my client base three-fold in four years.

"The second major aspect of my experience has been in the marketing of new stock issues, particularly in the resources area with junior issues. This work has ranged from the design of the marketing plan for Highspec Energy Corporation during my employment with Fastalk Securities to the soliciting of new development ventures with unlisted resources companies while I worked with Getinquick Resource Financing. In the first case the marketing plan was adopted nationally by my firm, resulting in a record distribution of stock. In the second case I was able to recruit seven new ventures for our junior portfolio, increasing the company's cash flow by three percent.

"The other major area in which I have been involved is supervision and training. This started in my first job with Windfall Securities, where I trained new brokers in basic securities selling techniques, and continues in my current position as Assistant Manager with Getinquick Resource Financing where I supervise an office of twelve brokers and support staff. There I have developed a fast method of training brokers involving a type of apprenticeship with senior brokers, thus saving the company the services of a full time trainer. In my present supervisory job I have cut staff turnover among brokers and support staff alike by more than twenty-five percent.

"So, although I have worked for four financial houses over the past fifteen years, the experience I have gained has mainly been in the three areas of selling, business development, and staff management, with responsibility for each increasing from one employer to the next."

Note how Jack has used an advance organizer (three major areas . . .), his accomplishments, and a summary (so, although . . .) to drive home the major points about his experience. He has cut across his experience, organizing the information he wants the interviewer to remember.

It is evident that this summary of Jack's experience does not include everything about him. He has selected aspects of himself more likely to ring the bells with a prospective employer. He tells what he thinks the interviewer wants to hear—and does so in a way that ensures it will be remembered.

The method that Jack uses to answer this question allows him a lot of latitude—much more than a chronological answer would. It allows him to highlight the aspects of his jobs that are most in line with the job he is seeking, whether or not such aspects form a major part of his current or previous jobs.

This approach also allows Jack to color the description of his previous jobs, using words that are in line with the job requirements of the position he is seeking. He can make himself sound tailor-made for the job, as if he had already done the same kind of work for a variety of other employers. Obviously you must be cautious not to carry this approach on too far. Do not attempt to make a prospective employer think you are thoroughly experienced in an area in which you have no experience—you will probably get caught.

Since the question of your experience is asked—in one form or another—in virtually all interviews, there is no excuse not to be prepared for it. Begin that preparation by identifying abilities or skills that cut across your experience. Try to think of several different labels for each skill so that you can vary the words you will use based on the skills likely to be viewed positively by a prospective employer. Do not forget nontechnical skills, those that allow you to do your technical job efficiently.

In the space below write down the summary skills you would highlight if asked to describe your abilities. As well, try to think of some alternate words you might use to describe the same skill. Try to group your answer into no more than four or perhaps five areas, because the interviewer is not likely to remember more than this. The first example is done for you.

Summary Skill   **Other Names**

1. *Interpersonal Effectiveness*   a. *People Skills*
                                     b. *Negotiating*
                                     c. *People*
                                         Management

2. _____   a. _____

                                     b. _____

                                     c. _____

3. _____   a. _____

                                     b. _____

                                     c. _____

4. _____   a. _____

                                     b. _____

                                     c. _____

5. _____   a. _____

                                   a. _____

                                   b. _____

                                   c. _____

THE GOOD, THE BAD, AND THE UGLY

Very often you are asked about your personal characteristics in an interview, particularly in an interview conducted by a professional interviewer. This question may take the form of, "Tell me about three of your most positive personal characteristics," "Why should we hire you?" or "What would someone who knew you well consider to be your greatest strengths?"

This type of question is a golden opportunity, although once again most people do not answer it to full advantage. Usually they recite, in either an embarrassed or overdone manner, a litany of easily ignored adjectives. Most, for instance, indicate that they are "good with people," "energetic," "a good team player," or "creative." Trouble is, those that are definitely none of these things often say the same thing as those that are. Being conservative, most interviewers discount or ignore such answers, even if they are true.

The best method of answering this question is similar to the method you used in designing your resume or writing your action letter. It does not rely on someone believing you. It relies on you providing evidence—your accomplishments—that precludes the listener from not believing you.

Janice Fastype was asked in an interview to describe the most important personal characteristics she would bring to a new job. After a considered silence of a few seconds she replied.

"I've always thought that there are three main personal characteristics that stand me in good stead in any job I do.

I'm not sure of how to describe the first one, perhaps stick-to-it-ness is the best description. When I was employed with Amalgamated Paper, I was the first secretary in a new area. I had to set up office procedures, order equipment, and work very independently, setting my own schedules and monitoring my own performance. My boss used to tell others that he could ask me to do something and then forget it. I was quite proud of that.

"Another thing about me that seems to benefit any company with whom I'm employed is the way I relate to people, both clients and fellow employees. When I was first employed with Neversleep Battery Corporation, I was assigned to the executive secretarial group, an area characterized by very high secretarial turnover because of the demanding interpersonal and technical climate. I worked for six different executives on a contingency basis. When permanent positions became open in five of these areas, I was offered the jobs. At the same time I was selected to represent the secretarial group in discussions with management about how the group could be reorganized for better efficiency.

"The other characteristic is related to my stick-to-it-ness. It's what you might call organizational abilities. I seem to thrive in an atmosphere that requires me to do several different things at the same time. In my current position with Neversleep Battery I'm responsible for organizing the time and requirements for the vice president and her two assistants. This involves international and national travel arrangements, supervision of two junior secretaries involved with a very heavy correspondence load, composing of standard replies to one hundred–plus internal and external inquiries per week, and confidential secretarial correspondence. I devote about thirty minutes at the start of each day to scheduling my day's activities. This has allowed me to be very precise with managers in telling them when jobs can be expected to be finished that day—because nothing gets lost in the shuffle.

"More than anything else, I guess it's these three things

185

that have helped me to be successful in what I do at work."

Never talk about a positive characteristic without backing it up with a specific example or accomplishment. Otherwise you will not be believed.

As well as positive characteristics, some interviewers will ask you questions that focus on your soft spots, personal areas that may hinder your performance or are relatively underdeveloped. This type of question is usually paired with a question about your strengths and may be stated as something like, "How about the other side of the coin. What are some personal areas that are less well developed or areas that you are still working on?"

This type of question is not a call for you to confess all of your sins, although some interviewers may prefer that you do so. The worst thing you can do in answering this type of question is to be brutally honest about yourself. For example if you know that one of your weaknesses is motivating and monitoring staff performance you would be foolish to tell that to the interviewer—at least in that form.

You must be careful in answering this type of question. You do not want to imply to the interviewer that you have no weaknesses—that will just make the interviewer think that you are arrogant and give him insufficient time to think of another question. On the other hand you do not want to be too truthful. Your honesty may be appreciated—but someone else will get the job offer.

There are two things to keep in mind in answering a weakness question. The first thing is to avoid mentioning a weakness that has a direct impact on the job you are seeking. By the time you have targeted your prospective employer, written your action letter, and found out about the position from a variety of sources, you will probably have a pretty good idea of what they are looking for—and what they want to avoid.

If you feel that you are weak in one of the areas critical to the position, it is better not to mention it. Focus instead on weaknesses that are not really weaknesses at all, those that have less impact on the job or ones that everyone has to some degree. Such weaknesses might include time management, being too hard-nosed in supervision, or getting too involved in your work. Once you identify the area you are going to concentrate on, you will want to consider how you are going to talk about the weakness.

In talking about the weakness you have decided to profile, you will want to discount the importance of that weakness and show how you have risen above it to realize your accomplishments. That way the accomplishment will be remembered—not the weakness. This is done by relating the weakness more to the past than the present and by showing that you have been working on the problem and are enjoying some success. Here are two examples.

"I think one of the areas that's troubled me in terms of work has been that I've sometimes gotten too involved in what I was doing. I would live the work—at work, at home, or wherever I was. I used to think that was good, that it showed commitment, but I think it also made me lose perspective because I was always into it. What I've been trying to do over the past three years is to schedule my work better, to set a time to do something—even if it's to worry—and to detach myself during other periods such as when I'm at home. What I find is, because I'm fresher and at least partially recharged, I can do more when I break things down that way. I wish I could say that I've completely dealt with that problem, but I have made very significant headway. I still have to keep on top of myself to make sure I don't slip back."

"I think if you talked with some of my employees, particularly when I first became a manager, they would tell you that I was too hard-nosed in my supervision techniques. Perhaps that was true because I did ride some of them pretty hard in making sure that the job got done.

I've had to reevaluate that position over the past few years and found that there are better ways to be hard-nosed—perhaps less obtrusive ways. I still expect a fair day's work for a fair day's pay, but I have mellowed somewhat in dealing with those who are generally good performers. I've been reading more about management techniques and am finding that there are other ways to achieve what I want to achieve. It seems to be having some results—I haven't had a single staff resignation in my area for the past six months and morale seems to be improved. I still have to keep watching myself because it's easy to slip back into your old ways.

Never talk about a negative characteristic without discounting its importance and showing that you are aware of the problem and are successfully working on it.

MONEY

You may be asked a question in interview that deals with your salary expectation for the new job. If possible, it is to your advantage to forestall answering this kind of question. It is to your decided advantage to talk salary *after* you have been offered the position since you will never be in a stronger negotiating position. Talking about it before that time increases the likelihood that your salary requirements will be a determining factor in whether or not you will be offered the job.

If you are asked a question about your salary requirements, say something like, "I'm not saying that salary isn't important as far as I'm concerned, but it's only one thing I look for in a new position. The most important thing, as far as I'm concerned, is the opportunity and the chance to do what I'm good at." If you are pushed further say, "I would expect to be paid the market level for a position of this responsibility, but I'm not sure I know enough about the job just yet to know what that would be. Let me put it this way—if we're both agreed that I'm the best person for this job, I can't envision that we'll find salary an insurmountable barrier."

INVASIONS OF PRIVACY

Although it is uncommon nowadays, particularly in larger organizations familiar with civil or human rights legislation, you may be asked questions that infringe on your right to privacy. Questions dealing with your marital status, your spouse or children, or other personal preferences are still asked in some personal interviews. This is most likely to happen if you are a female and are applying for a junior management position. What should you do if you are asked such a question?

It is unlikely that you will be asked a blatant tell-me-about-your-sex-life type of question. Unlikely, but possible. If you are asked such a question, it is probably to test your reactions, to see how you perform under pressure. Your first response should be something like, "I don't discuss that sort of thing in interviews." Resist the urge to give the interviewer a good dressing down, demonstrating that you are cool under pressure but are not about to be bullied. If asked again, or if the interviewer reaffirms that the question is real, repeat your first statement, but try to remain cool.

There is a natural tendency to want to blast the company whose interviewer asks such a question, a tendency that is very justifiable at the emotional level. And you now may have decided that you would not want to work for such a company even if you were offered a job. Before you do, remember that the interviewer may not represent the company as a whole and that you may be throwing away a perfectly good job opportunity because of one idiot. However, if you have made such a decision, stand up, saying something like, "Thank you for the interview, Mr. Jones, but I'm somewhat less interested in employment with XXX. I should tell you that I intend to press formal complaints as a result of questions you have asked in this interview. Good day." Once you leave, make careful notes about what questions you were asked, particularly the offensive questions. Then write a letter of complaint to the organization's CEO. If you receive no response within a respectable time, pursue your case with your local civil or human rights organization.

Most offensive questions are far less blatant and are often asked by the inexperienced interviewer because of ignorance of good interviewing principles and techniques. For a female questions sometimes asked include, "Are your children in school?" or "Do you have child care arrangements for your children?" It may be that you do not find such questions offensive or an invasion of privacy. If that is the case, you can simply answer them. On the other hand you may find such questions too personal and may be reluctant to answer them directly.

If this is the case for you, ask yourself what it is the interviewer really wants to know. In the cases above it is clear that the interviewer is worried that your children may have a detrimental effect on your work performance. Your potential work performance is a legitimate concern on the part of the employer—your children are not. Answer such questions in a pleasant manner that gets at the real issue. For example, you might say, "It sounds like you are concerned that there may be things in my personal life that may prevent me from doing a good job. Let me assure you that I have always made it my policy to arrange my personal affairs so that they do not adversely affect my job." In this way you address the real concern (performance) but do not allow for an unwarranted invasion of your privacy.

In dealing with questions that are embarrassing or invasions of privacy, make it clear that you will not be bullied. But do so in a pleasant and professional manner.

WINDING UP THE INTERVIEW

Interviews do not last forever—even if it sometimes seems like they do. The onus to terminate the interview is usually in the hands of the interviewer, and you should be sensitive to when the interviewer would like to conclude your session. Usually the cue for the end of the interview will be when you are asked if you have any (further) questions or when the interviewer elaborates on the next stage(s) in the selection process. At this point you should be prepared to say or ask something—even if there is no question you are burning to ask.

When you are asked if you have any further questions, hesitate for a moment, look pensive, and ask a question that gets at your understanding of what they are looking for in the position. Say something like, "Based on our discussion, it seems to me that you are looking for someone who has sound interpersonal skills, has a solid grasp of supervisory principles, and is not afraid to make decisions under pressure?" This is an implied question and should receive an answer from the interviewer. It will help to reinforce in the interviewer's mind the skills that are required—and that you are the person with these skills. I do not have to tell you that the characteristics you mention ought to be the ones you have already demonstrated by your accomplishments. If you have to *tell* the interviewer that you have these skills—do not—you will not be believed.

Conclude the interview by thanking the interviewer for talking with you and making certain that you know how the recruiting campaign will progress from this point. If this has not already been made clear by the interviewer, ask. You might say something like, "Can you give me some idea as to when you expect to progress in this recruiting assignment? When might I expect to hear from you again?" Remember to say something positive—not flattery—and thank the secretary or receptionist when you are leaving.

MORE LETTERS

Once you have arrived home after your interview, do not expect to sit back idly and wait to be summoned for a job. You should immediately write thank you or reinforcement letters to the interviewer and every other important person you met at the company during your interview. These letters should reaffirm your interest in the job and reinforce positive characteristics you demonstrated during the interview. A sample of both types of letter is given for Janice Fastype, the secretary described in the section on interviewing.

247 Dexterity Cres.
Manyfingers, North America
Ph. (555)555-5555

January 12, 19XX

Mr. Herman Alwaysright
Director of Personnel
Wow, Inc.
555 Demanding Road
Indenture City, North America

Dear Mr. Alwaysright,

Thank you for extending me the courtesy of a personal interview yesterday for the Executive Secretary: Support Services position. I appreciated the opportunity to find out more about this career opportunity with Wow, Inc.

As I indicated in our meeting, I am very interested in this position because it allows independent action and requires a good deal of organizational acumen. These skills were required in my position as managing secretary for a large foodstuffs company and I have found that I am most productive in such a work atmosphere.

You indicated in our meeting that you would be selecting a finalist candidate for this position in the next week. I look forward to hearing from you then.

Once again thank you for your interest in me for this position.

Sincerely,

Janice Fastype

247 Dexterity Cres.
Manyfingers, North America
Ph. (555)555-5555

January 12, 19XX

Ms. Damion Careershot
Project Assistant: Support Services
Wow, Inc.
555 Demanding Road
Indenture City, North America

Dear Ms. Careershot:

Thank you for taking the time yesterday to fa-
miliarize me with the Support Services Department.
I appreciate the first-hand exposure to your department; it helped me put into perspective the
position description that I had discussed earlier
with Mr. Alwaysright.

I look forward to meeting with you again should my
candidacy for the Executive Secreatry: Support
Services position be successful.

Sincerely,

Janice Fastype

From planning your answers to typically asked questions to
reinforcing a positive impression through follow-up letters, the
byword for interview success is *organization*. If you are
organized you will impress the interviewer in subtle ways,
ways that are not directly related to *what* you have said but
rather the authority and confidence of *how* you have com-
municated. This authority and confidence will go a long way
towards ensuring that you will be successful in your interviews.

Chapter 15

Miracles and More Miracles

"Trials never end of course. Unhappiness and misfortune
are bound to occur as long as people live, but there is a
feeling now, that was not here before, and is not just on
the surface of things, but penetrates all the way through:
We've won it. It's going to get better now. You can sort of
tell these things."—*Zen and the Art of Motorcycle Maintenance* by Robert Pirsig

Although it may seem as if it is never going to happen, sooner
or later you will get a job offer. If you have been doing
everything right, you may even get several at the same time.
That is an advantage for you—switching things from a buyer's
to a seller's market. You are in demand and it is time to make
the best out of what you have to sell.

It is likely that your job offer will come by telephone rather than
letter. This is done so that, if you refuse outright, the employer
will be able to contact a second choice immediately. If you
agree to the telephoned job offer, this is usually followed up by
a formal written offer to which you should respond in writing.

Not to immediately decline or accept the job offer is to your
advantage—even if you want the job very badly. Thank the
caller for the offer indicating that you are very interested in the
position, but that you would like a few days to think through all

the implications or to discuss it with your spouse. Try and get as much information about the offer as you can. If you are unclear about the salary offered, other benefits including relocation costs, or have any other questions—ask. Do not argue, quibble, or negotiate with the caller when you are initially phoned with the offer.

When you are offered a job, you are in the best position you will ever be in to negotiate the terms of your employment.

Your aim in going through the job search maze was to present yourself in the best possible manner as someone the employer would like to hire. In managing your presentation, you have probably not paid enough attention to your own concerns should you get the job. You may have appeared only minimally interested in salary and other benefits, promotion possibilities, or level of responsibility. Now that you have an offer in hand, you will want to evaluate your prospective employer in the same way as the employer has evaluated you. How good will they be for you? They want you but do you really want them?

Arnold was employed as a senior accountant with the head office of a successful chain of dry goods stores. He sought other employment after he realized that his chances for internal promotion were minimal.

Arnold ran his job search campaign very well—almost too well! After an intensive three month program he was able to garner three job offers within a single week. Although he was sorely tempted to jump at the first one he received, the best offer turned out to be the last one. Because he had allowed himself time to consider his options, he was able to select the one that best met his needs. He politely declined the first two offers—after he had the third one in the bag.

TURNING THE TABLES

If you have any doubts about your prospective position, it is to your advantage to request another interview. Rather than focusing on selling yourself in such an interview, your focus should be on gathering the additional information you will need to make the career decision that is in your best interest. In many ways you will be interviewing them, ensuring that there will be no surprises once you have burned your old job bridges.

A good way to arrange this interview is to telephone your prospective employer twenty-four to forty-eight hours after you have received their initial telephone offer. Indicate that you have had the opportunity to think through their offer, are still very interested, and would like to get together with them again to discuss a few details and to get a bit more information about the position. If you would like to meet with other people, perhaps some prospective co-workers or other managers, request that you be able to do so at that time.

Although it is common for employers to pay expenses incurred for your first interview, there is less consistency of approach regarding a second one. If the position you have been offered is a senior one, it is likely the employer will offer reimbursement of expenses. For more junior positions this may not be the case. If you have any doubt and if the amount is sizeable, ask.

There are several things you will want to be clear on after you complete your post-offer interview. They can help to form the basis for questions you will ask during your meetings.

1. It is likely your job offer was accompanied by a salary offer. Find out how that level was determined and where the salary is in terms of the range for that position. It is far better to be at the bottom of one range than the top of another if the salaries are roughly equivalent.

2. How will performance be assessed in your new position? What incentives are there for outstanding performances? Are there regular salary review procedures?

3. What latitude with staff will you have in your new position? What expectations does your new employer have for your first six months of employment?

4. What power will you have for unilateral action and what

will you have to accomplish in concert with others. Do you know or have a feeling for these "others?"

5. What career changes are possible from this position within the organization? What jobs within the firm does this position feed?

6. What skills does this position require that you may not already have developed to a high level? What type of assistance will the employer provide for this development?

7. Is there a probation period within which you can be terminated without cause or recourse?

8. What benefits, including relocation expenses, will be available to you?

In asking questions during this interview, guard against appearing too self-interested. As well, it is best if you can avoid the usual embarrassment that most people feel when discussing money or personal conditions. Try to approach the issue in a matter-of-fact manner.

Your job offer was probably accompanied by a specific salary or salary range. Usually there is some room for negotiation, depending on how badly the employer wants you. To make sure that you are being paid at a fair level, research what salary positions offer in similar organizations or, if possible, how this salary compares to other salary ranges paid by your new employer for jobs with similar levels of responsibility. If everyone who works with your new employer is paid less than average, you are unlikely to get a great deal more.

Bring up the topic of salary in a matter-of-fact manner, the same way you would approach any other topic. Indicate your strong interest in the position and let the employer know what you have found out by your research. Do not be embarrassed to indicate the salary range you would consider fair. At the very least if the salary offered cannot be modified try to get an agreement to have it reviewed in six months—after the company has had the chance to see you perform.

If this is an especially sensitive area for you, write out the questions you want to ask and have a friend role-play the situation with you. The time and effort will be very well spent because it could make a big difference in your salary!

After you have met with your prospective employer, but before you leave, reiterate your interest in the position and indicate that you have only a very few details to consider before you can let them know your decision. Arrange to call them within one to two days with your final decision. Whether you accept the position or not, follow up this call with a letter. If you accepted the position, your letter may be written in response to a formal offer mailed to you after you have accepted the telephoned offer. If a written offer is not to be exchanged, your written acceptance is especially important because it will detail your understanding of the conditions of your employment. A sample of such a letter written by Janice Fastype follows.

247 Dexterity Crescent
Manyfingers, North America
Ph. (555) 555-5555

January 24, 19XX

Mr. Herman Alwaysright
Director of Personnel
Wow, Inc.
555 Demanding Road
Indenture City, North America

Dear Mr. Alwaysright:

Thank you for meeting with me yesterday to discuss your offer of employment for the Executive Secretary: Support Services position with Wow, Inc. I appreciate your detailed description of the offer provided during our meeting and I am pleased to accept the conditions you outlined. As I understand it, those conditions are.

1. The starting salary will be $18,500 per annum. This is subject to a review within six months based on performance. Thereafter, salary reviews are done annually.

2. Relocation expenses, up to a maximum of $3,300, will be provided.

3. Starting date for this job will be March 1, 19XX, and there will be a three month probation period.

4. My immediate supervisor will be Ms. Damsel Indistress, although I will be reporting to Ms. Damion Careershot for that part of my duties involving the projects group.

5. A general statement of my job duties and responsibilities is included in the job description already provided to me by your office.

I look forward to my employment with Wow, Inc. I will contact you when I am in Indenture City to arrange accomodation.

Sincerely,

Janice Fastype

There is a natural tendency, once you have won your job, to forget about career planning. That is a mistake. It is not necessary to undergo perpetual gut wrenching self-analysis to ensure that what you are doing still meets your needs but you should not forget about the matter either. Certain aspects of career planning, particularly marketing your skills when the time comes to change your job, are best done on an ongoing basis. That way, you are less likely to forget what you have to sell.

THE ACCOMPLISHMENT LOGBOOK

There are really two kinds of information you should collect on an ongoing basis. Collect, that is, if you want to avoid sorting through the dark caverns of an aging memory when you really need the information. The first kind of information is your accomplishments; the second is your feelings about these accomplishments. An Accomplishment Logbook can help you put both kinds of information together painlessly.

There is nothing complicated about an Accomplishment Logbook. It requires you to collect, on an ongoing basis, the same kind of information you needed to complete the exercises in *CareerScan*. Here is how it is done.

1. On a regular basis, monthly or weekly depending on your work circumstances, write down what you have accomplished over that time period. As in the exercises you have already completed in *CareerScan*, these need not be earth shattering in their significance. What is important is that the examples be specific, singular, and that they include some indication of how well you have done what you have accomplished.

2. For each accomplishment you cite, write down which technical and nontechnical skills were required to do the job.

3. Indicate which personal need(s) were met by each accomplishment you have completed.

USING YOUR ACCOMPLISHMENT LOGBOOK

Your logbook can be an effective aid to career decision making. If you have kept a careful record of what you have accomplished, you are always in the position of being able to verify your skills. This is helpful in applying for new positions, promotions, or even in surviving your yearly performance appraisal. An annual or semiannual look at your accomplishments, and how you felt about those accomplishments, can help to ensure that your work will remain meaningful to you—as well as being a real morale booster.

In work if you know where you have been, you are more likely to know where you are going.

Grayson, a forty-five-year-old engineer, completed a career development seminar. Over the course of the next three months he considered four different offers of employment. He eventually accepted the offer from a mid-sized consulting company because it allowed for a mixture of high level design and management.

During the three years he was employed with the consulting firm, Grayson worked on a variety of projects, many involving a variety of skills, most undertaken as part of a team.

Grayson kept a careful record of what he had done during his three years' employment. It helped. He had evidence to support his growing feeling that the job was not for him—it did not meet his needs. It also provided him with the evidence he required to establish his skills and successfully market them to another employer—and to gain a new job more in line with his needs.

SECTION III: SUMMARY

1. The most important thing in searching for a job is to control the positive information about yourself that you release to a prospective employer.

2. Controlling negative information about yourself is very important to job success.

3. To be successful in searching for a job, you must identify what you have to sell a prospective employer and then sell it.

4. In searching for a job, you must provide information that will cause prospective employers to form positive inferences about you.

5. Do not use a resume as your first written approach to a prospective employer—use an action letter.

6. Your resume should be more than a series of job descriptions; it must tell what you have accomplished that will make you in demand for your new position.

7. Successful interviews are exercises in successful information management. Build up the positive and diffuse the negative.

8. Help the interviewer to remember important points about you. Remember what you are selling.

9. Successful negotiation is best left until you are offered the job.

Conclusion

Successful career management is not complex but it does require ongoing effort. With the help of *CareerScan* you have sharpened your awareness. If you have been having problems in your career, it is a better than even bet that these problems center on decision-making: What are you going to do? How are you going to do it?

Remember, to be successful in your career you do not need to know where you want to end up—the proverbial question of what you want to be "when you grow up." You need only know that what you are doing now meets your needs now. If you commit yourself to nothing else, commit yourself to working at that which satisfies you. Enjoy what you have but remain open to other opportunities that expand your possibilities for needs satisfaction.

A successful career is one that you control—one where you make decisions that are in your best interests. Such decisions are never easy. Nor are they made without regret for other roads not taken. Ultimately what will determine your success is your courage to decide in spite of uncertainty, the courage to act on the basis of maybes.

If you free yourself from the millstone of life goals, you free yourself from much of what stops you from making effective career decisions. With a life goal as your touch-stone every career decision is overdramatized, every decision bringing you one step closer to—or farther away from—where you think you want to be. With the present—your current prospects—as your basis for decision-making, you are free to act. And to be successful, act you must.

If you have read *CareerScan* this far, you already know what to do. Now do the smart thing. Put the book back on your bookshelf and start doing.

Good luck.

INDEX